The Hart Reguardant

Hertfordshire County Council 1889–1989

Gillian Sheldrick

First Published in 1989 by Hertfordshire Publications, County Hall, Hertford

Copyright © Hertfordshire Publications 1989

ISBN 0 901354-51-1 hardback

ISBN 0 901354-50-3 paperback

All rights reserved. No part of this publication may be reproduced, stored in a retrieval system, or transmitted in any form or by any means, electronic, mechanical, photocopying, recording, or otherwise, without the prior permission of the copyright holder.

British Library Cataloguing-in-Publication Data

CIP Catalogue Record for this book is available from the British Library

Published in association with Wheaton Publishers Ltd. A member of Maxwell/Pergamon Publishing Corporation PLC

SALES

Direct sales enquiries to Wheaton Publishers Ltd, Hennock Road, Marsh Barton, EXETER EX2 8RP Tel. (0392) 74121

Typeset by P&M Typesetting Ltd, Exeter, Devon

Printed and bound in Great Britain by Vine & Gorfin

CONTENTS

Preface	4
Introduction	5
1 The Foundations	7
2 Tentative Beginnings 1889–1918	13
3 Growth and Consolidation 1918–1945	31
4 Confidence and Expansion 1945–1974	55
5 Reassessment and a New Beginning 1974–1989	78
6 Contrasts 1889–1989	111
Appendices	
1 Chairmen of the County Council 1889–1989	114
2 Chief Officers of the County Council 1889–1989	116
Bibliography	122
References	125
Index	127

Preface
by the Chairman of Hertfordshire County Council

When discussions on the centenary of the Hertfordshire County Council first took place there were many ideas and suggestions about what could be done to celebrate the event. This book is one of those ideas which has developed into reality; for that we owe the author, Gillian Sheldrick, our gratitude.

I am aware of the research, effort and time that is involved in a work like this. It is a book which will become a reference for those who follow on in the next 100 years, helping them to learn from our experiences and to build on our achievements.

Fred Peacock BA FRSA JP
CHAIRMAN OF THE COUNTY COUNCIL

Members of the County Council with the Clerk outside County Hall in March 1974, just before the 'old' County Council gave way to the 'new'.

Introduction

In 1989 the Hertfordshire County Council celebrates its 100th birthday. The Council's work affects the lives of every one of us resident in Hertfordshire and, with the other local authorities, serves to complement the powers of central government. It is a body of men and women – currently 77 of them – elected by the adult residents of Hertfordshire. The councillors meet in full Council four times a year and much more often than that in committees for particular purposes. They have the duty to provide for everyone who lives in the county a wide range of services, which are paid for mostly from rates levied on Hertfordshire householders and partly from government grants derived from taxes. The day-to-day work of providing these services is carried out not by the elected councillors, but by the Council's 42,000 employees (including about 12,500 teachers) who work in premises all over the county.

The Council exists to serve the public, so in describing the first hundred years of its work, I have concentrated on developments in the services it has provided over the years, rather than on the politics and personalities of the Council itself and I have attempted to show what the Hertfordshire County Council has meant to the people of Hertfordshire since 1889.

In doing so, I have divided the life of the Hertfordshire County Council into four 'ages'. From its birth in 1889 up to the end of the First World War the infant Council gradually acquired more powers and experience, but had not yet achieved its full stature. During the next 27 years, to the end of the Second World War, the County Council gained strength and grew in self-awareness and moved into the first home of its own. It used the confidence gained in this period to expand and grow after the war in what was arguably its golden age, its responsibilities increasing and its opportunities seemingly endless. Then after 1974, the period of major growth came to an end and the Council entered a time of financial retrenchment and less certainty as to its role. It realised that it was not eternal and saw many of its contemporaries failing in their struggle for survival, and since then it has had to reassess its life and work. But though the Council may now seem middle-aged, or even elderly, it has achieved wisdom and experience in its maturity, and enters its second century in excellent health and spirits.

Although each of the four main chapters of the book deals with different aspects of the County Council's work during the period, generally corresponding to brief histories of different departments, I have been selective, and not every aspect of the Council's work is necessarily covered in detail for each period. Nor does the amount of space dedicated to each department in any way reflect its relative importance, whether on financial, social or any other grounds. My intention is not to provide a complete catalogue of everything the County Council has achieved during the last hundred years, but rather to provide a flavour of what its work has meant to the people of Hertfordshire throughout the period.

In writing the book, I have incurred many debts of gratitude: first, to the County Council itself, which (quite apart from providing me over the last eight years with a most enjoyable and rewarding job!) has now invited me to write this account of its history. My colleagues in the County Record Office and in the County Local Studies Collection have been enormously helpful, even when the centenary celebrations, which almost all of us were involved with at some time in at least one of their many aspects, began to produce more groans than smiles. All the Chief Officers and many other officers of the County Council have been most helpful in providing information, answering queries and checking the draft manuscript. It would be impossible to name them all, but I am nevertheless most grateful, and I should particularly like to thank the Chief Executive, Morris le Fleming, for the time he has devoted to the project. I would also like to thank the Chairman of the County Council, Fred Peacock, together with County Councillors Frank Cogan, Charles Bowsher and Michael Colne, who have spared the time to share with me their experience as members of the Council. Nigel Longmore and Bill Moralee have also provided me with essential background information. Arthur Jones, editor of Hertfordshire Publications, has helped, advised and encouraged and he and many other friends and colleagues have read and commented on various aspects of the manuscript: my thanks especially to Stephen Doree. My family and friends have seen little of me during the writing of the book, except for the thankless task of helping me move house in the middle of work on it, and I thank them for their forbearance. To all these, and to many others who have helped in some way, I am most grateful.

Gillian Sheldrick
DECEMBER 1988

1

The Foundations

Local Government for Hertfordshire before 1889

The new county councils which came into existence throughout England and Wales in 1889 had centuries of experience of local government on which to build. From the time of the Norman Conquest, monarchs had appointed 'shire-reeves' (sheriffs) to act as royal deputies and make the national government effective at a local level. Until 1576, a sheriff was normally appointed to act jointly for Hertfordshire and its eastern neighbour Essex. The sheriff had his own deputy known as a bailiff in each of the smaller administrative units known as hundreds, of which there were eight in Hertfordshire. Bailiffs ceased to exist as the significance of the hundreds as administrative and judicial units declined, but a High Sheriff (with limited and largely symbolic duties) is appointed to this day.

On a lower level, but much more relevant to the daily lives of the inhabitants of Hertfordshire's many villages, was the manor, a unit which might consist of one village, part of one, or two or more adjacent villages. From the eleventh century until at least the sixteenth, it was through the manors and their courts that agriculture in the village and the surrounding countryside was organised, the building of houses regulated, markets and fairs run and the quality of bread and ale checked. As an organ of local government, the manor lost most of its power centuries ago, but as a legal entity it existed into the twentieth century and in some cases retains a vestigial existence today.

The parish began life as a unit for purely ecclesiastical purposes, but from the sixteenth century it began to take over from the manor as the smallest unit of local government. The two most significant early civil functions imposed by law upon the ecclesiastical parishes were the maintenance of highways running through the parish and the relief of the poor, including the care of the sick and aged. Both these duties were regulated by central government during the sixteenth century and from then parish administration became both more wide-ranging and more highly organised. Each parish had to appoint surveyors of the highways, and everyone was required to work on the roads for a certain number of days each year (or to pay for a substitute). Overseers of the poor were also appointed, and their duties soon came to include arranging apprenticeships for poor children and orphans and in many cases running the parish workhouse – there were 48 parish workhouses in the county by 1776. Rates were levied on local residents to pay for the services provided by the parish government and in some parishes the members of the vestry, the parish's ruling body, were elected by the inhabitants, as members of local authorities are today.

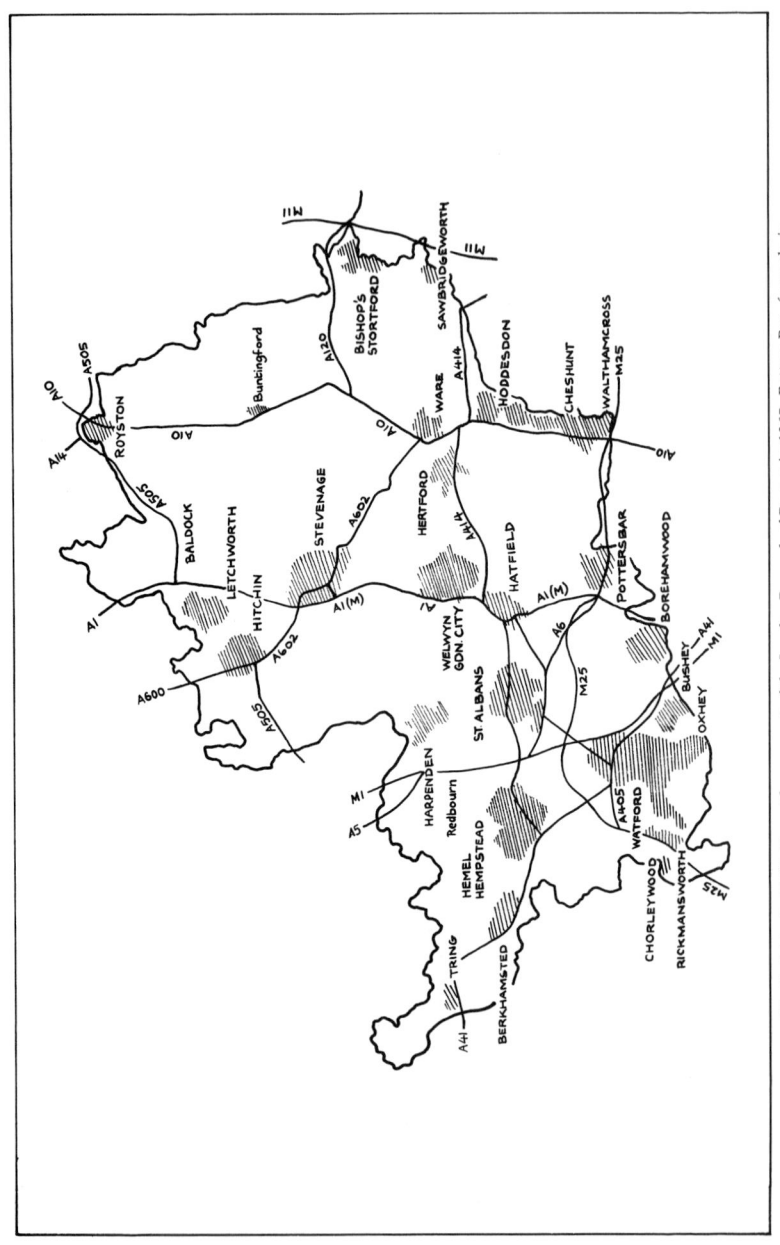

Hertfordshire in 1989. Barnet became part of the London Borough of Barnet in 1965. Potters Bar, formerly in Middlesex, was transferred to Hertfordshire in the same year.

The Nineteenth Century

By the early nineteenth century many rural parishes were too small to cope with the enormous expansion of public services which was such an important feature of the Victorian age, and larger units had to be created, each generally for one particular purpose only. The first and arguably the most important were the Poor Law Unions created in 1834 by combining groups of parishes into larger units intended to make more efficient the administration of poor relief. Hatfield Union, for example, consisted of the parishes of Essendon, Hatfield, North Mimms and Northaw. The Hertfordshire unions did not all contain only Hertfordshire parishes. Of the twelve Hertfordshire unions, Barnet, Berkhamsted, Bishops Stortford and Royston included parishes from adjacent counties. Unlike many of the ad hoc bodies of the time, the unions' ruling bodies, the Boards of Guardians of the Poor were elected by the local inhabitants. The union administration was so effective that many duties unrelated to the administration of poor relief were given to the guardians as the nineteenth century wore on – registration of births, deaths and marriages, enforcement of attendance at school, the assessment of rating valuations and so on. The unions were, indeed, so successful that they continued to exist alongside the County Council until 1930.

The rising population and increasing urbanisation of the Victorian age – the population of Hertfordshire alone doubled between 1811 and 1891 – together with a growing concern with the physical and moral welfare of the country's inhabitants also led to the creation of local authorities to improve public health: providing water, disposing of sewage, providing effective drainage and cleaning, paving and maintaining streets. Local Boards of Health were established in certain towns (in Hertfordshire, Local Boards were established between 1850 and 1874 for Baldock, Barnet, East Barnet, Bishops Stortford, Cheshunt, Hitchin, Stevenage, Tring, Ware and Watford) and in the rural areas Rural Sanitary Authorities were established in 1872. These covered the same combinations of parishes as the unions, and were, in practice, often run by the same group of people.

Other types of local authority were set up during the nineteenth century for specific purposes, including Highway Boards which provided and maintained roads in a group of parishes combined into a highway district. The best known, though, are probably the School Boards established in 1870 to provide schools in parishes where the provision of elementary education was inadequate. These boards had elected members, though in the case of the Highway Boards only some of the members were elected by local ratepayers; the rest were local justices, appointed by the Crown.

For centuries before the creation of the Victorian local authorities, the larger towns had had their own local government. Hertford and St Albans were old-established boroughs with a long tradition of self-government, quite separate from either the manorial, parish or union systems. In 1835, the Municipal Corporations Act reformed borough government, which in some areas had become notoriously corrupt. The most important provision of the Act was that establishing for each borough an elected borough council. Two-thirds of the members of each council were elected for a term of three years by the ratepayers of the borough, while the remainder were aldermen, elected by the councillors themselves for a six-year term. This was the first time that the principle that all the ratepayers of a particular place had the right to choose those who spent their money had been generally acknowledged by Parliament. When county councils were created over 50 years later, not only this principle of election by the ratepayers, but even the constitution of the councils, followed the pattern established for the boroughs.

Quarter Sessions

The direct predecessor of the County Council was, perhaps surprisingly in view of its mainly judicial role, the Court of Quarter Sessions. It had a very long history. Justices of the Peace were first appointed in Hertfordshire in the fourteenth century and from 1350 the justices for each county were obliged to meet in session at least four times a year (hence the title 'Quarter Sessions'). In Hertfordshire, there were separate Quarter Sessions for the boroughs of St Albans and Hertford until 1835, and for the Liberty of St Albans (consisting of 24 Hertfordshire parishes mainly in the south and west of the County) until 1874. The 'County' Quarter Sessions served the remainder of Hertfordshire – that is, excluding Hertford, St Albans and the Liberty – and each of these areas was, in effect, a separate administrative unit within the county. As well as acting as a court of law, the justices dealt with a wide variety of administrative matters. This was particularly true after the sixteenth century, for as the parish developed as the smaller unit of local administration, the county developed as the larger.

The duties of the Court of Quarter Sessions included supervising the repair of roads and bridges by the parish, and direct responsibility for the repair of certain county bridges; checking the quality of bread and ale; supervising the accuracy of weights and measures; regulating fairs and markets and licensing public houses. Quarter Sessions was the body to which appeals against the parish's administration of the Poor Law were addressed and as time went on, more duties were assigned to the justices in Quarter Sessions. From 1774, for example, they had the oversight of private lunatic asylums.

Quarter Sessions also initiated the provision of services, as well as regulating them. In 1841 the County Police Force was created (under the County Police Act 1839), though Hertford and St Albans each had their own forces, established in 1836. The new Three Counties Lunatic Asylum (now Fairfield Hospital) which opened in Arlesey in 1860 was built by co-operation between the Hertfordshire, Bedfordshire and Huntingdonshire Quarter Sessions.

The justices did not, of course, usually carry out all this administrative work personally. From the time of their first appointment in the fourteenth century, there was a Clerk of the Peace to act as a sort of chief executive officer to the justices while in each hundred the Quarter Sessions had two officers called High

Constables. Below them each parish had a Petty Constable. Much of their work was concerned with policing as we understand it today, but much was administrative – the petty constable was, for example, often the rate collector for the parish.

By the nineteenth century the Hertfordshire Quarter Sessions had developed a committee structure which was to be imitated and developed by the early County Council – until today almost all of the enormous amount of work and policy-making handled by the County Council is dealt with by specialist committees and sub-committees, not by the full council. In 1799 a 'Visiting Justices' Committee was created to report on the County Gaol and House of Correction. From the 1820s a Finance Committee was appointed, and became a permanent committee in 1835. By 1869 there were four permanent committees: Finance; Visiting Justices; County Constabulary and a Committee of Visitors to the Three Counties Asylum.

The provision of local services costs money, and this was as true of the services provided by Quarter Sessions as it is of those provided today by the County Council. Although there were some government grants available for special purposes, almost all the expenditure of Quarter Sessions was met from rates paid by local residents and assessed as a proportion of the value of their property. In 1888, the last year of its existence as an administrative body, a rate of 1¼d (0.52p) in the pound was levied, and the expenditure was £15,683. This excludes expenditure on the police and lunatic asylum, for which there were separate, smaller rates. Although Quarter Sessions continued to act as a judicial court until 1971 when the court system was reorganised, 1888 was its last year of existence as an administrative body, for in the following year the Hertfordshire County Council was created.

Members and some officers of the first Hertfordshire County Council, which assumed responsibility for the administration of the county on 1 April 1889.

2
Tentative Beginnings 1889–1918

Unlike some shire counties which contain a large regional centre of population, Hertfordshire has for centuries been characterised by the presence of a number of medium-sized towns such as Hitchin, Ware, Bishops Stortford, Berkhamsted and the county town of Hertford, and by 1889 over half the population lived in towns with a population of over 4,000. The biggest urban concentrations were in the south of the county, which was most strongly influenced by the nearness of London, particularly Watford (where over 20,000 people lived) and St Albans. Even so, Hertfordshire in 1889 was still essentially rural in character. The total population of the county was around 220,000 – around 0.5 people per acre, compared with a national average of around 0.8 per acre (today, the county averages nearly 2.4 per acre, much higher than the national average of around 1.3 per acre). A quarter of its working population was engaged in agriculture and related rural crafts. Hertfordshire's dominant crop was barley, grown for the flourishing malting industry, especially in the drier north-east. Other typical Hertfordshire crops included watercress (particularly in the west) and lavender (especially around Hitchin in the north) and vegetables for the London market were already being grown in the acres of glasshouses in the Lee Valley. A large proportion of the remaining working population was employed in domestic service, not just in the large country houses of the nobility and gentry such as Hatfield House or Panshanger, but also in every middle- and upper-class home and in a good many working-class homes too. The county's heaviest industry was paper-making, concentrated in the Gade Valley in west Hertfordshire, and dependent on the canals to transport raw materials to the mills and to carry away the finished product. Main roads north from London, especially the Great North Road, had long had a significant effect on the growth of Hertfordshire's towns, and by 1889 four main railway lines passed through on their way to the North, and in 1887 the Metropolitan line reached Rickmansworth, paving the way for the development of south Hertfordshire as a commuter dormitory.

When the County Council came into existence, there were already a number of lesser local authorities: the boroughs of St Albans and Hertford, together with Local Boards of Health, Rural Sanitary Authorities and Poor Law Unions. Boards of Highways were responsible for the upkeep of the roads in seven highway districts; while School Boards provided education in 21 parishes. However, the only authority with county-wide jurisdiction was the Court of Quarter Sessions. Towards the end of the nineteenth century it was becoming obvious that the wide range of administrative bodies created for special purposes could no longer cope efficiently with the increasing duties being thrust upon them. In addition, ratepayers were increasingly paying for local services over which they had no means of control. In 1889, as a result of the Local Government Act of 1888, 50 county councils were established to cover the whole of England (with twelve more for Wales). The administrative counties thus created did not always coincide with the 'historical' counties: the ancient county of Suffolk, for example, was given two councils. But the new Hertfordshire County Council had responsibility over the whole of the historical county of Hertfordshire, and no county boroughs (large towns with the status of a county) were created in Hertfordshire.

The constitution of the new county councils was based on that established 50 years before in the boroughs: each council consisted of a number of members (54 for Hertfordshire) elected by the county electors, who served for three years, plus County Aldermen (up to one-third of the number of elected councillors) chosen by the council, who served for six years. A chairman, serving for one year, was chosen by the councillors and aldermen. Although the new councils were elected by residents of the county, not everyone had the right to vote. Basically, the franchise was limited to heads of households who were ratepayers, and although women (who could not vote at all in parliamentary elections until 1918) were permitted to vote, very few were able to qualify. To be eligible to stand for election, the qualifications were similar, except that until 1907 women were not permitted to stand. In 1918, wives of electors became eligible to vote if they were over 30 (the age was reduced to 21 in 1928). Until 1945, though, non-ratepayers were excluded: the parliamentary franchise was wider than that for counties. People who paid rates in more than one area – for example shopkeepers who lived in a different area from their shop premises – had more than one vote; this was the case until as late as 1969.

The establishment of electoral divisions was carried out by Quarter Sessions, which divided the county into 51 electoral divisions, of which the Borough of Hertford was to be represented by two County Councillors, the City of St Albans by two and the remaining divisions by one each. At the elections for the first Hertfordshire County Council on 17 January 1889, only 22 of these 54 seats were contested, and the contests were not fought on party lines. As a local commentator wrote in the Hertfordshire Mercury[1] 'politics have wisely been almost entirely excluded from consideration, and in many cases the candidates have been nominated by members of both parties' [ie Liberal and Conservative]. Elections remained non-political until well after the First World War.

The members elected were typically from the upper classes, and at least a third of them had already served the county before as Justices of the Peace, like John Evans, member for Abbots Langley, who was Chairman of the Quarter Sessions. Their numbers included two peers and a viscount, together with three Members of Parliament. Of the rest, around a third described themselves as 'gentleman', or 'esquire' and another third were involved in trade, mainly malting or brewing, although those who, like Evelyn Simpson, member for Baldock, described themselves as 'brewer', were engaged in manufacturing only

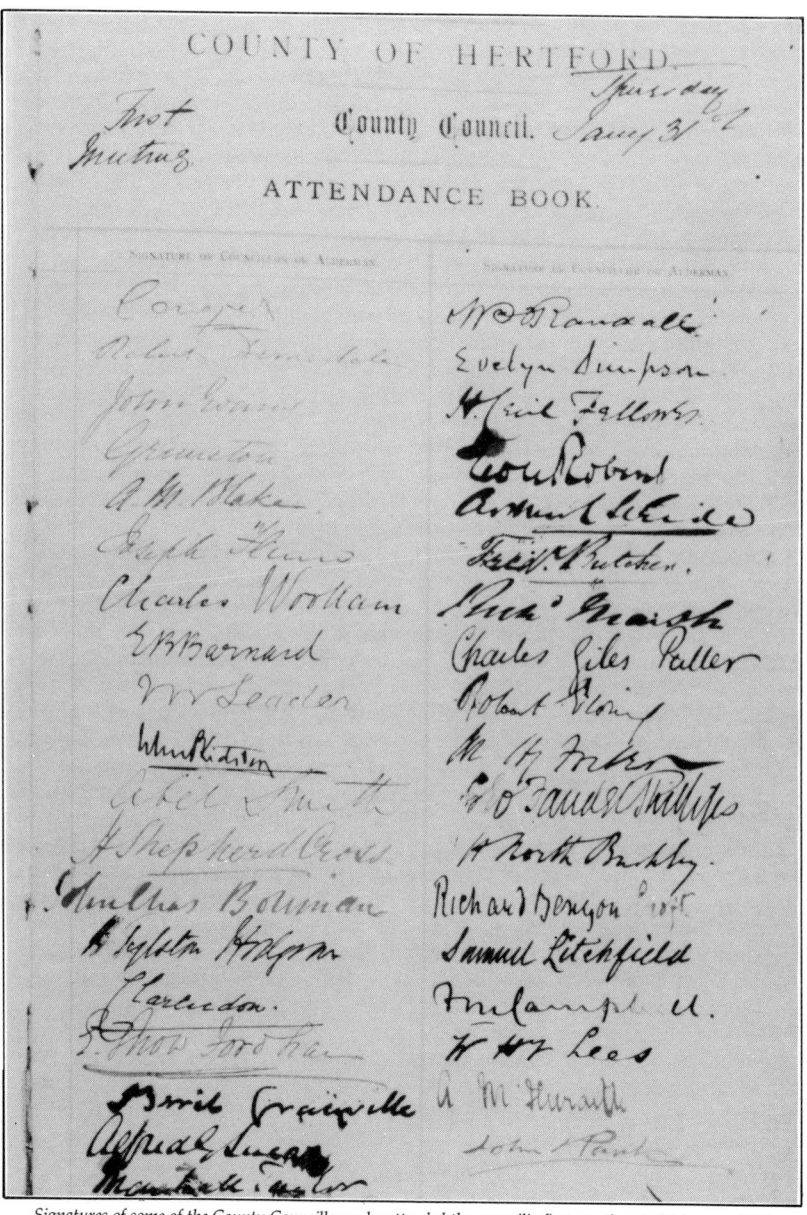

Signatures of some of the County Councillors who attended the council's first meeting on 31 January 1889.

as owners and managers. Another peer, the Prime Minister Lord Salisbury, was chosen by the members as an alderman.

The first meeting of the Council took place on 31 January in the Shire Hall at Hertford where it was welcomed by an official address from the Borough of Hertford (composed and read by the Town Clerk, Charles Elton Longmore, who was also the County Treasurer). It expressed 'gratification that [the first meeting] is held in this our County Town' and assured the new Council that 'we contemplate with considerable satisfaction the fact that the system of Local Government which we have enjoyed in this Borough for upwards of half a century, has now been extended to the County. We feel convinced that having regard to the constitution of your council the ratepayers are justified in looking forward to an efficient and economical management of their local affairs at your hands.'[2] It is significant that this statement implies what was generally felt to be the case, that the new Council's job was not to innovate nor to improve the condition of the county's inhabitants, but merely to carry out the minimum of essential duties as cheaply as possible.

At the first meeting, the eighteen County Aldermen were chosen, together with the first Chairman, Earl Cowper, who was to hold office until 1901. The second meeting was held at the Court House in St Albans (where the Council received a second address, this time from the Mayor and Corporation of the City of St Albans), and it was agreed that meetings should be held alternately in Hertford and St Albans; it would be another 50 years before a permanent meeting place for the Council was established. It was not until the Council's third meeting, in March 1889, that it ceased to discuss its own internal affairs and began to consider its wider duties, into which it would enter on the day it officially took over the administrative affairs of the county: 1 April 1889.

The duties of the new County Council were varied, but extremely limited compared with those exercised by it today. It had to maintain main roads and bridges; manage (together with the county councils of Bedfordshire and Huntingdonshire) the lunatic asylum at Arlesey (now Fairfield Hospital); provide a police force (run jointly with Quarter Sessions); ensure the accuracy of weights and measures used throughout the county; ensure that food and drugs were not adulterated; and look after the county buildings (mainly the Shire Hall at Hertford and the Court House at St Albans). In addition, there were more minor duties such as issuing music and dancing licences and explosives licences and duties under the Diseases of Animals Acts. The administrative and policy-making work required to carry out these duties was not carried out by the full Council of 72 members. Six committees were appointed, each responsible for one area of the Council's work. The Highways Committee, for example, dealt with roads and bridges and other matters connected with roads and transport. This delegation to committees was to a certain extent inherited from Quarter Sessions, but the County Council used the system much more extensively.

As more duties fell to the County Council, so more committees were appointed. Today, the County Council and its committees are little involved in day-to-day decision-making, such as the titles of new books to be stocked in its libraries or the colour of paint to be used in a new school; their work is much more concerned with wider issues of policy, such as whether a new bypass is to be built, or whether a new school can be afforded. In its early days, though, committees were much more involved in making the most trivial decisions. The County Buildings Committee, for example, discussed the very routine maintenance of buildings belonging to the county, so that when in June 1899 the Town Clerk of St Albans wrote to complain of the insanitary condition of the urinals at the Court House, the committee considered the problem carefully before directing the County Surveyor to discuss with the Mayor of St Albans the best way of remedying the nuisance.[3] All the committees met in London, at a variety of locations including the Inns of Court Hotel and the Law Society's Hall; it was much easier to travel to London by train than to cross the county from east to west.

Since 1865 the post of Clerk of the Peace had been held by Sir Richard Nicholson, a solicitor with offices in St Albans and London. In 1889 he was also appointed Clerk to the Hertfordshire County Council, and continued to serve in both capacities until 1894. Nicholson also held both these posts for Middlesex and was Clerk of the Peace for London; he retained his Middlesex and London posts until 1913. The employment of a solicitor as clerk to a public body was not unusual at this time, but the number of important appointments held by Nicholson was probably unprecedented. After his resignation in 1894, the post of County Clerk was transferred to the Hertford solicitor, (Sir) Charles Elton Longmore who had been County Treasurer since 1879, and in whose family the clerkship was to remain until 1948. The County Council's major financial post, County Accountant, remained in London until 1939, with the firm of W B Keen.

A County Surveyor had been appointed by Quarter Sessions to organise and plan the road and bridge maintenance programme, and he also became responsible for buildings and other works. The position had been held since 1876 by Urban Smith, and he was reappointed to the same post by the new County Council. His offices, like those of the County Accountant, were in London, and at first this was not seen as any handicap to his carrying out his duties efficiently. However, the work of the County Surveyor increased so much that in 1899 he gave up his firm's private practice work and became a full-time county officer. The County Council took over his London offices, but in 1901 the department moved to new offices in Hatfield.

The expenditure of the first County Council was tiny: at £106,000 per annum in the early years it was less than 0.02 per cent of today's annual budget of around £600m (gross). About a third of the Council's income came from local rates and the remainder from 'assigned revenues' – the proceeds of various taxes and duties such as probate duty (paid when a will was proved) and public house licences, the income from which was allocated to local government. Because county councils were considered by central government to be little more than a necessary evil, they received only a small proportion of national resources. However, as they took on more functions and duties, county council finance had to be placed on a less haphazard basis. More government grants for specific purposes (such as education) were paid, and by 1929 had almost completely replaced the assigned revenues.

The characteristic response of central government in the nineteenth century to new problems of local admininstration had been to create a new type of local authority for each new function. With the creation of the county councils, which were followed in 1894 by the 'third tier' urban and rural district councils, it became the norm to give new functions to these existing, general-purpose bodies, and the old single function authorities were gradually wound up. By the time of the First World War, Hertfordshire County Council had taken on responsibility for education and a wide range of medical services, though it had yet to enter the fields of welfare and the administration of the poor law, town and country planning and fire protection.

Roads and Bridges

One of the most important functions the County Council inherited from the Court of Quarter Sessions was the maintenance of the county's main roads and bridges. At first, the county was only responsible for about 200 miles of roads. More and more roads were accepted by the county as 'main' roads, so that by the turn of the century, nearly 1,000 miles of roads were the responsibility of the county (today, the County Highways Department maintains 2,600 miles of roads). In 1889, the number of bridges for which the county was responsible – 129 – was also tiny compared with today's 1,700 bridges. Many other bridges in the county were maintained by private owners or by district or parish councils, and as the years went by many of these were adopted by the County Council.

The County Council's main concern in respect of roads was in the essential business of ensuring that the county's traffic – mainly horses and carts, but with an ever increasing number of motor vehicles – could travel from place to place quickly and efficiently on well-kept roads and could cross rivers and streams safely. There were, however, other matters for its attention too. In 1898, for example, the Council made bye-laws requiring vehicles to be lit when travelling on highways at night. The Motor Car Act of 1903 imposed a general speed limit of 20mph (the limit had previously been 14mph), and county councils could reduce the limit to 10mph in particular places. The County Surveyor and Chief Constable agreed that 20mph was too high, and 'in many of the narrow streets and lanes Motor Cars should proceed at a considerably lower pace than ten miles an hour'.[4] They felt, though, that there was a danger of motorists assuming it was safe to travel at 10mph when they should really be driving much more slowly, and it was not until 1906, following an experimental period with no additional speed limits, that the first 10mph limits were imposed, mainly in towns. As well as marking speed restrictions, the County Council was also responsible under the Motor Car Act of 1903 for erecting signs warning of such hazards as dangerous corners, crossroads and steep hills. In 1904, 123 of the government's approved signs (a rectangular sign surmounted by the familiar red warning triangle) were bought for use at 78 places in Hertfordshire.[5]

The question of light railways, or tramways, was much discussed in the 1890s, for roads would have to be widened to accommodate any which were built. At one time, the County Council hoped that an extensive system of tramways would be the best way to connect the rural areas of the county, but it soon became clear that motor buses would, after all, be able to cope with the distances involved. Although several schemes were proposed, the only tramways ever built in Hertfordshire were on the fringes of London.

Police

Until the early nineteenth century, the upholding of law and order was, effectively, in the hands of the private citizen, though in rural areas the parish constable tried hard to keep order, and in some places Societies for the Prosecution of Felons were founded. In 1829 the Metropolitan Police Force was established, and this soon became the model for forces elsewhere. The Hertford and St Albans Borough Police Forces were both founded in 1836; the boroughs had actually been required to establish police forces under the Municipal Corporations Act of the previous year, but the County Police Act of 1839 merely allowed Quarter Sessions to create a police force to cover the remaining areas. Not until 1841 did the Hertfordshire Quarter Sessions vote to establish the Hertfordshire Constabulary. When the County Council came into existence in 1889, responsibility for the police force was vested in a Standing Joint Committee of the County Council and Quarter Sessions, which continued to exist until 1965. The Hertford Police Force was incorporated in the County Police in 1889, but the St Albans Police remained a separate force until 1947, and the southern part of Hertfordshire has always been within the jurisdiction of the Metropolitan Police.

Although the force began energetically in its efforts to establish law and order in what was still very much a lawless age, its impetus soon slowed down. In 1880, the second Chief Constable, Henry Daniell, was appointed, and he gave the force the new life it so much needed. One of his first steps was to adopt new methods of keeping accounts and reports, and to appoint a chief clerk to deal with all the paperwork – not very exciting, but an essential foundation if the force was to carry out its ever-increasing duties in an efficient manner. He also made sure that both the constables and the sergeants did actually carry out their proper duties, particularly the regular night patrols which had often been evaded. Reform was a gradual and continual process, and as late as 1899 the problem of regular night patrols was still being tackled. In that year, a prostitute was hacked to death in Railway Street, Hertford, despite several reports to the police station that a woman was being attacked and despite the fact that a constable should have passed the point of the murder on his regular nightly beat. As a result, Daniell introduced the system of half-hour congress points on all beats to make sure that they were being properly worked, and to keep track of all constables and officers throughout the night.

Many of the force's early problems were due to poor communications, and once the telephone was introduced these began to be solved. From 1891, telephone lines between police stations in Hertfordshire began to be installed, and by 1893 there were telephone links between Watford and Bushey, Watford and Rickmansworth, Watford and St Albans, St Albans and Hatfield, and St Albans and the Clerk of the Peace in Hertford. In 1895, married police inspectors, sergeants and constables at the telephone stations were asked if they objected to their wives answering the telephones. Even when the public telephone system began to develop, the police still had some private lines, so up to the First World War not all police stations could be reached from the public exchanges, and even as late as 1922 not all police constables (who of course in rural areas worked from their homes) were on the telephone.

Bicycles came into use in the Hertfordshire Constabulary later than telephones. In 1893 one was bought as an experiment at Watford and by 1896 the police owned eleven bicycles. In that year, officers were permitted to use their own machines for police work, with an extra allowance of 3d per hour for such a dangerous occupation! Every cycle trip was fully documented. Despite the caution surrounding the use of bicycles, they were used on quite a large scale, and it is probably because of this that horses were relatively little used by the Hertfordshire Police – in 1914 there were just thirteen horses and riders in the mounted section. In 1905 the force's first motor car (a Wolseley costing £225) was bought for the use of the Chief Constable. From 1911, the Chief Constable was permitted to hire cars as necessary, but it was not until 1914 that a car was bought for use by the police generally. As late as 1922 the necessity for having cars at all was questioned by the Standing Joint Committee, which proposed the reintroduction of horses and traps! Today, the Hertfordshire Constabulary possesses 377 motor vehicles, including cars, vans, motorcycles and other vehicles – but no horses.

From the earliest days of the Hertfordshire Constabulary, duties were sometimes carried out by ordinary officers in plain clothes, but with the nearby example of the Metropolitan Police, which had had a detective department since 1842, it seems surprising that a Hertfordshire department did not begin work earlier than 1892. In that year a plain clothes officer was appointed in Watford, which was the chief trouble-spot in the County because of its proximity to London and to London crime. Even so, the Hertfordshire Constabulary – like other forces – continued to rely on officers of the Metropolitan Police for detecting crime until the Hertfordshire Criminal Investigation Department was formally set up in 1911. The Metropolitan Police remained the source of much technical advice and assistance: it would not be until 1937, for example, that the Hertfordshire Police started its own finger-print and photographic department (using a disused canteen sink at headquarters).

Local Taxation and Licensing

The County Council was responsible for issuing a great variety of licences, including dog licences, game licences, gun licences, licences for places of entertainment and licences for cinemas. The issue of cinema licences from 1909 involved the inspection and approval of the premises, with particular reference to fire precautions, for the early celluloid films were extremely flammable. To a certain extent, the Council was also involved in ensuring that the films shown were acceptable. Films were not subject to censorship by the government in the same way as stage productions, but the British Board of Film Censors had introduced its 'U' and 'A' classifications in 1912, and from 1925 Hertfordshire County Council (following the example of London) made it a condition of licensing that no films other than those with a 'U' certificate were to be shown to children under sixteen unless accompanied by an adult.

The most important work of the County Council in this area, though, was to be the registration of motor vehicles and the issue of driving licences. Licensing of vehicles began in 1899, but it was the Motor Car Act of 1903 which began the system of registration still in force today, including the requirement for all drivers to hold a licence. Under the Act, every motor vehicle registered had to carry a plate bearing its registration number. Each registration authority used a different set of letters as an index mark – Hertfordshire's earliest vehicles were allocated the letters AR. The vehicles registered were recorded in great detail: in January 1904, for example, the Marquess of Salisbury registered a steam car (AR165) 'to seat four persons, black with dark green panels and gold lined'.[6]

Weights and Measures

The importance of maintaining fair trading practices, and particularly the use of accurate weights and measures, antedates the County Council by many centuries. Even Magna Carta declared in 1215 that weights and measures should be uniform and accurate throughout the realm, and ever since then efforts have been made to achieve this ideal. In 1495, for example, standard sets of weights and measures were made to be kept in 43 towns and cities throughout the realm (including Hertford); while in 1670 a standard bushel measure was ordered to be chained in every market square so that people could check the accuracy of their purchases of grain. A new set of standards was issued in 1824, and in 1835 a general system of inspection and verification was established, with Inspectors of Weights and Measures appointed by Justices of the Peace. The difficulty, though, was to enforce the standards. Even in the 1860s, a wide variety of measures were in use: the standard imperial bushel was 8 gallons, but in Middlesex a bushel of grain contained 8½ gallons; in Shropshire 9½ and in Cheshire 10. Many local measures with names like 'coombs', 'strikes' and 'hobbits' were still being used. It was the development of education, transport and the press, and the expansion of trade, which encouraged the acceptance of a standard system as much as legislation. In 1878, the inspection of weights and measures was put on a new footing, and for the first time there was central control over the inspectorate, exercised by the Board of Trade. This central control continued after 1889, though the inspectors were now appointed by the County Council.

In Hertfordshire, as elsewhere, the pre-1889 inspectors were normally police superintendents, but the new Standing Joint Committee of the County Council and Quarter Sessions considered that this was unsatisfactory. However, policemen continued to assist in checking the weights of loads of coal, and the Chief Constable acted as Chief Inspector of Weights and Measures until 1950. The county was split into two divisions (later increased to three), with headquarters at Watford and Hertford, and for each an Inspector of Weights and Measures was appointed (the City of St Albans had a separate Inspectorate, independent of the county, until 1974). Both the first two inspectors were previously inspectors in Leeds – the Inspector for the Eastern Division, W G Rushworth, served until his death in 1908 and he was succeeded by his son, who served until his own death in 1934. Although from the beginning the inspectors had duties in connection with the Food and Drugs Act and the Explosives Act, almost all their time in the early days was spent on the inspection and verification of weights and measures. A horse-drawn van was provided to carry the standards of weights and measures around the county, so that traders could bring their equipment for checking, and as this was so heavy, and wasteful of horse-power, a light cart was provided for the inspectors to travel on their general tours of inspection. The work load was not light: in 1894, 2,312 shops and other premises in the county were visited, out of 5,600 liable to inspection. As the population of the county – and hence the number of shops – grew, particularly in Watford, so did the work. In the year 1909/10, over 3,000 premises were visited out of 6,770 liable for inspection and nearly 55,000 individual weights, measures and weighing machines were inspected. (By 1987, the department's duties affected 20,000 trading premises in the county.) However, only a small proportion of these were found to be inaccurate, or illegal because they had not been stamped as verified, and in only 34 cases were traders prosecuted, for offences such as using unjust weights or not carrying scales on a baker's cart. An 'incorrect' weight is not necessarily 'unjust'; to be accurate, weights and instruments are expected to conform to the standard with a very fine degree of tolerance, and a slight deviation does not make it unjust.

Examination and sampling of food was another aspect of the Weights and Measures Department's work, which has grown in importance through additional legislation throughout its existence. In 1900, for example, as a result of the Sale of Food and Drugs Act 1899, more samples of food and drugs had to be taken for analysis: 250 per year throughout the county, instead of 120 as before. Even so, in many counties much more attention was paid to this aspect of the work. In 1905 the Board of Agriculture expressed concern at the low number of samples taken in Hertfordshire, which worked out at about 1.2 per 1,000 of population – the second lowest proportion in the country (Kent, for example, took as many as 5.4 per 1,000). The percentage of Hertfordshire samples showing that food was adulterated (for example, milk which had been watered down) was, on the other hand, extremely high, which was a great cause for concern – though it could also suggest that the inspectors were skilful in selecting samples of food which they suspected were impure. The range of goods examined grew ever wider as a result of Acts of Parliament or government regulations, such as the Sale of Butter Regulations 1902 (which defined 'genuine butter' as containing no more than 16 per cent water); the

Top; One of the county's standard measures of capacity in their travelling case. Bottom; Indenture verifying the accuracy of the county's standard weights, 1927.

Fabrics (Misdescription) Act, 1913 (prohibiting fabric from falsely being described as safe from fire, when in fact it was flammable – the Act was prompted by incidents of children burnt to death in flammable flannelette clothes); the Merchandise Marks Act 1926 (requiring certain imported foods such as meat and apples to be marked with the country of origin when offered for sale); or the Artificial Cream Act 1929 (under which artificial cream – usually made from butter, dried milk and water – was to be described as such).

The County Records

The importance of the county's written records has been recognised since the days of Quarter Sessions, though until relatively recently the concern of the county administration was almost exclusively for the records which it created or used. The Shire Hall in Hertford, built in 1768 by James Adam, contained a record room, with 'closets' for storing the records. By 1835 Quarter Sessions reported that these were in an 'insufficient state' and ordered that the papers and records were to be kept in tin trunks, and that the closets should be lined with tin and put in good repair. At the same time, it was decided 'that the Clerk of the Peace be directed to sort and arrange the records so that they may be inspected with more facility.'[7] The records had already been listed, and a list of the records stored in the record room in 1825 includes many items still used by visitors to the Record Office today.[8] In 1825, too, the Sessions records themselves were first indexed, to enable better use to be made of them.

The importance of the old Quarter Sessions and other records was not simply historical; then as now they were preserved primarily for legal reasons. In 1897, for example, the bridge at Cat Hill, East Barnet, was badly in need of repair. The inhabitants of the area refused to pay for the work, asserting that the bridge was a county one, repaired by Quarter Sessions in 1835, and that the County Council should therefore bear the cost of repair. A search in the Quarter Sessions rolls revealed no reference to the bridge having been repaired at the expense of the county, and the bridge was declared not to be a county bridge.[9]

The County Council addressed the question of the county's records from its early days: a Records Committee was appointed in 1895 'to consider and report upon the question of the County Records, and as to the best means of arranging and keeping them.'[10] It was most unusual at this time for a County Council to pay such attention to its records, though neighbouring Bedfordshire was another pioneer, appointing a records committee in 1897. In 1900 the Hertfordshire Records Committee agreed to adopt the recommendations of a meeting of the influential Congress of Archaeological Societies held in London in March 1900. The congress had endorsed suggestions made by a government committee on local records, including that for a country-wide network of local record offices run by the county councils – a system which even today is incomplete. As William Le Hardy remarked of these recommendations in his preface to the *Guide to the Hertfordshire Record Office* (itself now nearly 30 years old) 'it is interesting to note that although sixty years old they are in accordance with modern practice' in their acceptance of the principles that local record offices should be provided, with competent staff as custodians of the records, that they should accept deposit of manorial records, private papers and ecclesiastical records and that the records should be made available for inspection by students.[11] In pursuit of these ideals, a strong-room to house the records was built in 1909 in Castle Street, Hertford. The one-storey building, containing three record rooms, was secure and air-conditioned (the air being filtered, warmed and dried before coming into contact with the records); security from fire and theft, a clean and non-static air supply and a constant temperature are still the most important criteria for good records storage today. The original strong-room, enlarged in 1930, still stands, though it ceased to be used for records storage in 1952, and the Record Office's public search room, offices and main storage areas were transferred to the new County Hall in 1939.

Cataloguing and publication of the records was at first undertaken by Hardy and Page, a firm of record agents – experts in searching old records whose expertise was mainly employed by solicitors. Hardy and Page's first duty, in 1895, was to report on the county records in the Shire Hall in Hertford – where they were found in ten cupboards, twenty tin trunks and loose on floors and shelves – and in St Albans, where they were mostly stored in the Court House, and it was suggested that they be brought into one place for safe keeping. The Records Committee then decided they should be sorted and listed (by Hardy and Page) and cleaned and bound (by Stephen Austin of Hertford). The publication of 'calendars' (that is, summaries and extracts) of the Quarter Sessions minutes and other records began in 1905, the tenth and final volume being published in 1957, and by 1920 a complete catalogue, or explanatory list, of Sessions records was completed.

The firm of Hardy and Page (in effect W J Hardy, who died in 1919, followed by his son William, who later adopted the name Le Hardy after tracing his Channel Islands ancestry) would serve the county until 1946. In that year William Le Hardy became the first County Archivist, referred to until 1950 as the 'County Records Officer'; the appointment was a part-time one until 1957, since Le Hardy also held the post of County Archivist of Middlesex.

Health

The Hertfordshire County Council inherited from Quarter Sessions some involvement in what today have become the health and social services. Chief of these was the running of the Three Counties Lunatic Asylum near Arlesey, opened in 1860 and shared with Bedfordshire and Huntingdonshire. The accommodation provided by the Three Counties soon proved inadequate, and at the end of the century Hill End Asylum, near St Albans, was built.

In 1897 a County Medical Officer of Health was appointed to co-ordinate the fight of district medical officers against disease and such aspects of public health as poor drainage. Some of his problems are familiar still today. One fifteenth of deaths in Hertfordshire in 1901 (209 people) were from cancer, and the Medical

Medal presented by the County Council to Mabel Johnson for two years' perfect attendance at school.

Officer reported that this number was increasing. Although he admitted this was partly due to better diagnosis, he identified cancer as the greatest problem he had to face, partly because so little was known about it.[12] Other problems, though, are strikingly indicative of the progress which has been made: in the same year, nearly 300 people died from tuberculosis. Forty children died from measles, and over 100 from diarrhoea, mainly as a result of drinking tainted milk or water. From 1908, the county was responsible for carrying out regular medical inspections of school children, and this helped to identify such health problems as malnutrition as well as poor eyesight or vermin.

Mothers too became the responsibility of the County Council. From 1903 midwives had to be inspected and registered by the County Council, so that by 1910 no unregistered midwife could attend a birth except under the direction of a qualified medical practitioner. By 1905, 111 midwives had been inspected and registered. A large proportion of these were untrained; thirteen were illiterate and several of those who could write could not or did not keep proper records of their work. In addition, as the Medical Officer reported, 'some of those who have been practising for years have extremely antiquated appliances' which they were not always careful to sterilize or even to clean.[13] In 1906, a Lady Inspector of Midwives was appointed, who from 1911 was also County Health Inspector. As well as undertaking more extensive inspections of midwives, including making surprise visits, she co-ordinated the work of health visitors and promoted health education, visiting mothers' meetings to give a series of 'Homely Talks on Health' and addressing girls' clubs on 'the subject of personal hygiene'. The local health visitors and midwives also carried out this educational work, and by 1911 at least one 'school for mothers' had been established in the county, though unfortunately in reporting on its existence, the Lady Inspector did not say where it was.[14]

The County Council was not empowered to employ midwives and health visitors itself, but instead it promoted the formation of the voluntary County Nursing Association, which came into existence in 1908, and the various District Nursing Associations. The associations provided trained nurses, and particularly midwives, to women who could not afford an independent private nurse, though at first they mostly had a rule that only 'respectable married women' could be attended. With 243 illegitimate births in 1905, the Inspector of Midwives expressed concern in 1906 that this meant that unmarried mothers – often young girls forced to resort to the workhouse – would 'fall into the hands of less reputable women'.[15] The County Nursing Association also trained nurses, opening its Training Home at Watford in December 1908, and the County Council awarded four County Midwives' scholarships to enable girls to train there, on condition that they practised in Hertfordshire for two years after qualification.

Education

During the nineteenth century, education had become available to more and more children, through the schools established with the help of the National Society for Promoting the Education of the Poor in the Principles of the Church of England (founded in 1810) and the British and Foreign Schools Society (founded in 1811 and mainly associated with the nonconformist churches). Education had been theoretically available to all children since 1870, when a School Board was set up in each parish where there were no school places, or not enough. Since 1891 elementary education had been free and from 1876 it had been compulsory for children between the ages of five and fourteen to attend school, though children as young as eleven could be exempted under a complicated set of rules, which included passing examinations at a prescribed level and achieving a certain number of attendances. The rules varied from place to place, depending on the bye-laws made by the local education authority. In parishes in the Hertford Rural District, for example, a child was exempt from attending school if there was no school within 2 miles of his home or if at the age of twelve he passed exams at Standard V. He could also claim 'partial exemption' (ie could attend school for only part of the year – particularly significant where child labour was still used in agriculture) if at the age of twelve he passed at Standard IV *and* if he made 200 attendances per year, and five attendances a week between 20 October and 20 June *and* had made 300 attendances per year for the last five years. In Ashwell, to take just one more example, exemption could be gained from the age of ten by passing at Standard

Girls exercising at the Hitchen British School, c. 1900.

IV, while partial exemption at the age of ten required only 150 attendances a year and a pass at Standard II.

Although it was not until 1903 that the County Council became responsible for educating most of the county's children, it did have some involvement in education from the beginning. Grants were made towards the costs of a wide variety of classes which came under the general heading of 'technical instruction': classes in subjects as diverse as French, shorthand, beekeeping and nursing could qualify. Normally, though, most of the initiative in starting and running the classes was local, with the Council providing the money but not the expertise or administrative support. In Hitchin, for example, the classes were run by a joint committee of the members of the Mechanics' Institute and the Blue Cross Brigade. The classes there began in 1891 with joinery and woodcarving and by 1900 shorthand, first aid, nursing, woodcarving, book-keeping, building construction and cookery were being taught. In Cheshunt, the classes were run by a local Technical Instruction Committee and included cookery, dressmaking, French, wood-carving, agriculture and horticulture and 'ambulance' (ie first aid classes, run by the St John's Ambulance Brigade). From 1900, the Council became more directly involved in running classes and organised classes especially for school teachers.

Under the banner of technical instruction, the Council was also able to promote secondary education in the county, though once again it took little initiative at first in actually providing education. Grants were made to eleven grammar schools towards the cost of building works and for the salaries of teachers of certain subjects. The schools all charged fees, but the Council awarded scholarships to the county's brightest children. Even so, secondary education was a rarity: in 1904 only just over 1,000 children attended the public secondary schools – almost three-quarters of them boys.

When in 1903 (following the 1902 Education Act), the Council became responsible for elementary education as well, the number 'on the books' was around 47,300. Until then, most schools had been provided either by religious organisations or by the School Boards, of which there were 23 in Hertfordshire by 1903. In 1903 the County Council took over the board schools, though the church schools (known as 'non-provided' schools) continued to exist alongside the county ('provided') schools, and many still exist today as voluntary schools. In Hemel Hempstead, too, there were non-county schools, since the borough exercised its option under the Education Act (because of its population and its status as a borough, which it had achieved in 1898) to become a separate education authority for elementary education, a status it retained until 1945. Watford Urban District and the City of St Albans, which also qualified to opt out, preferred to become part of the county system.

Although the County Council's school attendance bye-laws which came into force in 1905 were more standardised than those previously in force, they still allowed for some variation in different districts: in most rural areas, children could leave school at twelve if they had passed at Standard V, with partial exemption for agricultural employment on passing Standard IV, while in some urban areas they had to reach Standard VII to leave at twelve, and Standard VI to leave at thirteen. During the First World War, when children's labour was used to supplement that of women, even these standards were often not enforced. It was not until 1918 that attendance up to the age of fourteen became universal. Under the same Act (Fisher's Act), the employment of children below the age of twelve was forbidden and children under fourteen were not allowed to work for more than two hours a day.

Even where attendance was theoretically compulsory, it was often difficult to enforce. The County Council continued the practice of the old School Boards and School Attendance Committees of offering prizes (or bribes) for attendance. These were not insubstantial. Before the First World War, for example, a child received a book for each year's perfect attendance, with a medal as well for two or more years' full attendance. Five years' full attendance qualified a child for a watch costing (in 1905) 18 shillings. In 1905, these watches were costing the County about £150 a year, so around 167 children a year had not missed a single day's school for five years. At a time when many people might otherwise never possess a watch, these prizes were much coveted, and although they may have encouraged attendance, there were many cases of children coming (or being sent) to school to make sure of the prize even when they were extremely ill, thus endangering not only their own health but that of the other pupils. From at least 1912, the Medical Officer of Health criticised the system on these grounds[16] and from 1915 attendance prizes ceased, though on the grounds of economy during the war rather than to protect children's health.

Agriculture and the First World War

The devastating effects of the First World War, unlike those of the Second World War, did not become fully apparent until the hostilities were over. Even so, as the war dragged on, it became obvious that the people at home were being affected by more than the loss of men at the front. Conscription of unmarried men began in 1916, but already most jobs were being carried out by those too old, too young or too unfit to fight, and women of all classes were for the first time employed on a large scale on other than domestic work. By 1917 there was a severe shortage of food, with queues becoming severe, and rationing – beginning with sugar – was introduced. Hertfordshire County Council had appointed a War Agricultural Committee (including agricultural experts as well as County Council members) in 1915 in order to encourage the efficient production of food. In 1917, with the government's Cultivation of Lands Order, its powers became more extensive and it had to appoint a separate Executive Committee (which worked independently of the County Council) to carry out a wide range of duties. The Committee carried out a survey of the county to ensure that land capable of being cultivated was not going to waste. Not only food, but seed too was scarce, and the committee acquired and distributed such commodities as seed potatoes. With fewer and fewer men to work on the land, the Women's Land Army was established, and the Agricultural Executive Committee was responsible for training its workers. In 1917, workers on the land, who had previously been considered more useful producing food than fighting, were called up for military service, and there was a massive campaign to recruit more women to take their place. From 1917, too, prisoners of war were employed in agricultural work – by 1918, 890 prisoners of war, based in fourteen camps, were at work on Hertfordshire farms.[17]

Its work during the war was not the first involvement of the County Council with agriculture; since 1908 it had owned land which was let as smallholdings of up to 50 acres. The experience gained during the war was, however, to have a lasting effect, for in 1920 the powers of the Executive Committee passed to the County Council's new Agricultural Committee, which in 1921 established the Hertfordshire Institute of Agriculture (now the Hertfordshire College of Agriculture and Horticulture) at Oaklands in St Albans.

On Armistice Day, 11 November 1918, the County Council held its meeting as usual in the Court House in St Albans. After reading and signing the minutes of the previous meeting, the Chairman (Sir Thomas Halsey, Bart) announced that he had 'received information' that the Armistice had been signed. The minutes of the meeting record that 'the announcement was received with much enthusiasm and the National Anthem was sung by the whole assembly. The Chairman then announced the news to the Public from the balcony of the Court House.'[18] The Council, having thus entered a new era, then proceeded with its normal business.

3
Growth and Consolidation 1918–1945

At the end of the First World War, the people of Britain emerged into a new society, a world which for the first time had been shaped by the experience of total war. Everybody, rich and poor, had suffered personal loss of sons or brothers, husbands or neighbours; everyone had experienced the shortage of food and the rationing introduced at the end of the war – though for the poorest the war had often meant better living standards and increased wages. The problems of poverty and malnutrition could no longer be ignored after the poor state of health of many of the army recruits had been revealed; there had been little or no improvement since the Boer War, when 40 per cent of recruits had been rejected because of poor health. Women had proved that they could carry out most kinds of work which men could do, and had discovered other occupations than domestic service. The upper classes realised that they could (and would have to) cope without armies of domestic servants to run their homes. Society was still unequal and class-ridden, but there had been much levelling.

In the immediate post-war years there was a short economic boom, with high wages and work easy to find, but by the 1920s, this had lost its impetus, and in 1929, with the collapse of the American stock market, the depression began in earnest. Between 1921 and 1940, there were never fewer than 1 million people in Britain without jobs, and between 1931 and 1935 over 2 million were registered as unemployed. The true number of those without work was even higher, since the official figures did not include married women, the self-employed or agricultural labourers. In Hertfordshire, however, the effects of the depression were cushioned. It was already a wealthy county and had none of the heavy industries which suffered most from the depression. People were better able than many elsewhere to afford to share in the increase of mass leisure activities now available such as motoring, the cinema (especially after 1927 when talking films appeared) and radio (public service broadcasting began in 1922). The consumer society had begun – the chain stores of Woolworths, Marks and Spencer and Sainsbury's were all established before the Second World War; and electricity became commonplace: the National Grid, with pylons carrying electricity all over the country, was virtually complete by 1933. Even the poor were better fed and clothed, and the sight of barefoot children became rare, though the classic cycle of poverty, with the elderly, the sick and those with large families suffering most, remained. Large families became rarer, though. The size of upper-class families had begun to fall at the end of the nineteenth century and working-class families, too, were now smaller.

Smaller families contributed to the better position of women. From 1918 women over 30 could vote in parliamentary elections, and from 1928 women over 21 (the same age as for men). Women were no longer legally barred from holding public office or appointments in the civil service simply because of their sex – though in the civil service at least they still had to leave when they married. By 1923 around 4,000 women in Britain served as magistrates, local councillors or members of Boards of Guardians of the Poor. By 1925 there were four women on Hertfordshire County Council – out of 80 councillors and aldermen. The first women police officers were finally appointed in this period. The idea of having women police constables in Hertfordshire had been suggested during the First World War, but it was not until 1928 that two women constables (two sisters) were appointed. In some cases, though, further restrictions were placed on women. Until 1923, the Hertfordshire County Council had not discriminated between married or single women applying for teaching posts, though of course it would normally specify whether a man or a woman was particularly required. Single sex schools were the norm, and a woman would be preferred to teach girls, though it was expected that men would have first choice of jobs which were available to them. In 1923 the Education Committee resolved that as there were more teachers than available posts, preference would be given to single women over those who were married. In the following year it was even proposed that 'all married women other than widows should be asked to resign their positions now held under the County Council', though this was not actually approved.[1]

For the County Council, the period was one of expansion and consolidation. Every aspect of its work saw growth: with the new importance of the motor car, the provision and maintenance of roads and bridges became ever more important. In education, thought began to be given to the provision of secondary schooling for those over eleven, and a reorganisation of schools took place on lines which foreshadowed those laid down in the 1944 Education Act. There were new responsibilities, too, such as the creation of the rural library service and new duties in the field of welfare services which the County Council took on in 1930. More services meant more staff and the need for a greater professionalism in its work. Professionalism and efficiency demanded central and permanent offices, and the most exciting achievement of the period was the erection of County Hall in Hertford, which was finished in 1939 and occupied on the outbreak of the Second World War, just as the Council embarked on its new wartime responsibilities.

Party Politics and the County Council

It was now becoming less and less possible for the elected members of the County Council to become involved in everyday decision-making. The role of the County Council increasingly became a policy-making one, as it is today, while its officers carried out the everyday work. With this emphasis on policy making came the beginnings of party political involvement in local affairs. In Hertfordshire, this did not really become significant until after the Second World War, though the Labour Party began in 1930 to contest County Council elections on party lines. In 1934 (the year incidentally in which the Labour Party took control of the London County Council), three Labour members were elected to the Hertfordshire County Council. Despite this, there appeared to be little enthusiasm for local elections amongst members of the public. In 1937, for example, only one-third of the Council seats were contested and many people did not bother to vote.

One of the most notable Labour members of the County Council at this time was George Lindgren (later Baron Lindgren), who entered the County Council in 1931. He had been educated at a London County Council elementary school and worked as a railway clerk, and was active in the trade union movement, in complete contrast to the majority of the County Councillors with their privileged middle- or upper-class backgrounds. Lindgren became leader of the Labour group on the County Council and was the county's first Labour alderman. Even after he became a Member of Parliament (for Wellingborough) in 1945, and served as Parliamentary Secretary in a variety of ministries, he remained a member of the County Council until his defeat in the 1955 elections.

In 1925, four of the members of the County Council were peers, one was the son of a peer and three were knights or baronets. Each of the six chairmen who served before and during the Second World War was either a peer, a knight or a baronet. It is indicative of the small amount of work involved in being chairman of the County Council at this time that for the first 50 years of its life it was served by only five chairmen, all of of whom were active at the same time in many other areas of public life. In the fifty years since 1939, the Council has had fourteen different chairmen, who have had to devote themselves more single-mindedly to the job. One of the most highly respected chairmen in the period between the wars was Sir Edmund Barnard. He not only died in office, but actually during a County Council meeting. Exceptionally, the full Council met in January 1930 not in Hertford or St Albans but in the Law Society's Hall in London, where committee meetings were often held. The main business of the meeting was to consider and adopt the scheme for the administration of the Poor Law by the Council, made under the 1929 Local Government Act. Barnard had taken a major part in preparing the scheme and himself moved that the scheme be accepted, but as the minutes record: 'While moving the above resolution, the Chairman of the County Council died suddenly and upon the motion of the Vice Chairman, the County Council immediately adjourned and no further business was transacted.'[2] The clerk, Barnard's great friend Sir Charles Elton Longmore, took the unusual step of publishing a verbatim transcript of the proceedings of the meeting, up to the point where the chairman died[3] – and he himself was to die shortly afterwards, possibly from illness contracted during Sir Edmund's funeral.

Other typical members of the Council at this time were Robert Woodhouse (a member of the Council in the 1920s and again after the war, and a County Alderman from 1949) and Sir Edward Beddington (a member from 1936, a

County Alderman from 1948 and Chairman of the Council 1952–1958). Both came from wealthy families, and in the 1920s Beddington lived in the extensive Hadham Palace, while Woodhouse's first action on moving to Bengeo Lodge, Hertford was to extend his house to accommodate comfortably his domestic staff as well as his family. Woodhouse was active in a wide range of public service, being particularly involved in hospital development, and in his post-war service with the County Council was particularly active on the Tuberculosis and Education Committees.[4] Beddington, however, appears to have viewed his position on the County Council as largely a ceremonial one, and in his memoirs, he appears to be prouder of his election as Chairman of the Puckeridge Hunt than as Chairman of the County Council![5]

Education

In 1918, most children in Hertfordshire attended a County elementary school until they reached the school leaving age of fourteen. Most of what is today called 'secondary' education continued to be provided by the elementary, or 'all-age' schools or by 'continuation' or evening classes for those who had left school. From 1918 the Council had a duty to provide secondary education for the more able children, but in general this was limited to making grants to existing grammar schools rather that providing new ones. In the late 1920s, a new impetus was given to secondary education. It is often assumed that the development of today's education system, with different types of school for children of different ages, with a change of school at (usually) eleven, began after the Second World War. However, in 1926 the Hadow Report *The Education of the Adolescent* advocated a system similar to that which was to be legislated into existence by the 1944 Education Act. It proposed a common education until the age of eleven, after which a child would proceed to the type of school most appropriate to his or her abilities and probable career: grammar school for the academic child, who would stay at school until sixteen or seventeen (admission by examination, fee-paying, but with scholarships available); 'central' or 'modern' school (free, but admission would be by examination) for those who wished to follow commercial, technical or industrial courses; and senior school (continuing the elementary school course) up to the age of fourteen for the remainder. There should also be 'junior technical schools' which provided vocational, training for those over fourteen. None of these types of school was new – modern schools had existed in London since 1911 and junior technical schools had been developing since the beginning of the century – but they were uncommon. In 1923 only 7.5 per cent of children in England and Wales attended a secondary or junior technical school.

Hertfordshire, like many other counties, adopted the new scheme with enthusiasm. In Watford, the reorganisation of schools along 'Hadow' lines, including the establishment of a junior technical school, came into force in September 1929, and reorganisation in other urban areas followed quickly. The

Children at Wilstone School engaged in pioneering craft work in 1939.

work of reorganisation was made more difficult and more urgent by a government instruction to ensure that senior classes contained no more than 40 children and junior classes no more than 50. The Council also had to provide new accommodation for children whose schools had been blacklisted by the Board of Education in 1925: seven Hertfordshire schools, including Bovingdon County Council School and Hitchin Queen Street British School, were said to be unsuitable for recognition by the board and incapable of improvement. In 1928, when the county drew up its plan for the 'formidable task' of reorganisation, as the Chief Education Officer described it at the time, there were 242 elementary schools in the county, variously organised into infant (5 to 7 or 8); junior (5 to 9, 10 or 11); general older (7 or 8 to 14 plus); and senior (9, 10 or 11 to 14 plus) departments. There were 121 senior classes with over 40 on roll, though all but 18 infant and junior classes contained fewer than the prescribed maximum of 50. There seem to have been few objections to the new educational system. There were complaints at Offley that the new senior school was too far for children to come home to lunch, but the provision of transport and school dinners seems to have satisfied parents. The new system involved a fair amount of new building, and new uses of old buildings, particularly to provide sufficient secondary places. In Hertford, for example, the grammar school (now Richard Hale School) was given brand new buildings, and the newly established senior school took over the old grammar school buildings. The first new grammar schools provided by the County Council were built : Letchworth Grammar School (now the County Council offices in the Broadway) and Hemel Hempstead Grammar School (now Hemel Hempstead School), the first co-educational grammar schools in the county. In general, and although some schools such as Waterford, Sacombe and Flamstead were closed in 1931, the Council adopted a policy of retaining the small rural schools where possible, believing that large town schools were not appropriate or necessarily better for the education of the rural child who needed 'an education suitable to his environment and probable future occupation'.[6]

Rural Libraries

By 1924, only the towns of Hertford, St Albans, Watford and Cheshunt had established library services, run by the Borough or Urban District Council, but in that year, the County Council resolved to establish a Rural Library Service. Hertfordshire was by no means first in the field – 21 English counties had already established rural library schemes, as they were permitted to do under the 1919 Public Libraries Act – but the service grew rapidly to serve a long-felt need.

The primary purpose of the new library service was to make books available in the many villages of the county, and it was on the rural areas that it concentrated at first. The first books were bought by means of a grant from the Carnegie Trust, and the work of the first County Librarian, William Pickard, was to send boxes of books at regular intervals to the many local library centres.

Top; *Ashwell Library Centre in 1948; one of the many voluntary libraries which received regular boxes of books sent by the County Library from 1924.* Bottom; *One of the county's first mobile libraries at Aldbury in the 1950s.*

These local centres were quite unlike today's branch libraries. Their librarians were unpaid volunteers and accommodation was provided wherever it could be found: in the village school at Knebworth; in the Post Office at Cuffley; in a room in the librarian's house at Watton-at-Stone; even in a draper's shop at Sandridge. The new library built at Bushey in 1935 on a site given free to the Council was very much an exception; until the 1950s it remained the only branch in the service housed in a building specially designed as a library. Opening hours, too, were very limited; one day a week was normal, and in some places the library was open for as little as an hour a week. In some cases (generally in towns), the local library had its own permanent collection of books, but in most cases the library was dependent upon the box of books sent out from Hertford and changed two or three times a year.

By 1930, after five years' work, the County Library's staff consisted of just the County Librarian and four assistants, and it had a stock of 49,455 volumes. Even so, it served 135 centres and had over 35,000 members. By the war years some urban libraries had permanent branch librarians, and in 1944 issues of books topped 2 million for the first time (today, issues top 13 million a year). The distribution of boxes of books to rural centres remained, however, the service's main function throughout this period and also its popular image.

Health

Health care was an important area of concern for the County Council in this period. Since 1908, Local Education Authorities had had to carry out medical inspections of schoolchildren, and in Hertfordshire School Medical Officers hoped to inspect each child three times in their school life. In 1920, for example, children entering elementary school were inspected, together with children born in 1912 (ie aged around 8) and those born in 1908 or leaving school before the age of 12 – 13,811 inspections in all, with 1,803 children referred for treatment for dental disease and 747 (mainly girls, with their long hair) for 'unclean heads' (ie lice). In 1938, 15,038 inspections were made, and 1,798 children were treated for dental disease, but only 38 for unclean heads – an indication that the campaign for improved health and personal hygiene was taking effect. In contrast, by 1968, 60 years after the regular inspection of schoolchildren began, 37,577 inspections were made, but by this time general health and standards of cleanliness had improved out of all recognition and the most common defect identified was no longer disease or vermin or malnutrition, but defective vision.

Another task of the Medical Officer and his assistants was the fight against tuberculosis, which was perhaps the 'typical' disease of the period. Until after the Second World War, the main cure was good food, fresh air, sunlight and rest, which were generally provided in specially built sanatoria. The proposal to build a County Sanatorium at Willian for the treatment of TB sufferers was first made in 1913, but the First World War interrupted the plans, and it was not until

1923 that the Ware Park Sanatorium in Hertford was opened instead. It continued to be run by the County Council until 1948 when, on the establishment of the National Health Service, it passed to the Regional Hospital Board.

The 1913 Mental Deficiency Act was, in the words of the Medical Officer of Health, intended 'to make better provision for the protection and control of ... mentally defective persons'.[7] This sounds rather hostile to the mentally handicapped people it was intended to help, but under the Act the County Council did manage slowly to improve the level of care. Kingsmead Special School in the buildings of the former workhouse at Hertford was opened in November 1919, to house and train for simple employment boys and girls categorised as 'feeble minded and higher grade imbecile, which may be regarded as educable or improvable'.[8] Many of these children benefited enormously from the care and special treatment they received. Older mentally handicapped people, though, were often placed in mental hospitals intended for the mentally ill, like the Three Counties Asylum, simply because until 1933 there was nowhere else for them to be looked after. In that year, the Cell Barnes Colony opened near St Albans, to provide specialist care and training for mentally handicapped adults. Even so, Cell Barnes was very far from today's ideal of mental health care in the community. It was originally planned to house 300 people, but was soon enlarged and by 1935 over 500 residents lived together in one large institution.

The County Council was also responsible for the health and welfare of babies and their mothers, especially after the passing of the Maternity and Child Welfare Act in 1918. From that date, the Council provided infant welfare clinics, ante-natal care and advice, health centres and day nurseries. It also ran a maternity home at The Maples, Hitchin and from 1938 the Watford Maternity Hospital. Health visiting was particularly important. In 1928, for example, ten years after the passing of the Act, 3,797 of the 4,526 babies which had been born in 1927 were visited by County Health Visitors. Ante-natal care was much less developed. In 1919, only 140 expectant mothers were registered with the clinics for ante-natal care, and even in 1928 only 475 were on the registers. It must be remembered, though, that in those pre-National Health Service days only the least well-off would have expected to have their health care provided free. One measure of the success not just of the ante-natal clinics, but of the Medical Officers' efforts at improving the general health of the nation, is the infant mortality rate (the measure of the number of children per thousand live births dying during the first year of life). In 1919, Hertfordshire's rate was the lowest ever for the county, at 49.5 per thousand – in 1917 it had been 67 per thousand. In reporting this, the County Medical Officer commented that 'this rate, however, would be further reduced if greater efforts were made to combat the chief cause of infant mortality, namely congenital debility. Ante-natal work and the giving of advice and instruction is ... of great importance in relation to the reduction of infant mortality.'[9] Ten years later that rate had indeed gone down to 45 deaths per thousand. In Hertfordshire today the rate is only 7.6 per thousand.

Welfare

For the first 40 years of the County Council's existence, most welfare services to those in need, including children, old people and the poor, had continued to be provided by the Boards of Guardians created in 1834 under the Poor Law Amendment Act. All were responsible for 'out-relief' to the needy not in institutions and for many patients in hospitals and specialist institutions, and some also ran hospitals, such as Wellhouse Hospital in Barnet. In 1930 Poor Law Unions were abolished and County Councils (or County Borough Councils, though there were none of these in Hertfordshire) took over the administration of welfare services. Under the County Council's new scheme, Hertfordshire was divided into seven areas, based on the old unions. For each area there was an Area Guardians Committee (technically a sub-committee of the County Council's Public Assistance Committee, but still with a good deal of independence) replacing the old Board of Guardians. The St Albans and Watford Guardians Committee Areas corresponded to the former Watford and St Albans Unions, but elsewhere pairs of unions were combined to form larger, more manageable, areas. Cheshunt (which had been in the Edmonton Union, based in Middlesex) became part of the East Herts area, and the parishes in Essex, Cambridgeshire, Middlesex and Buckinghamshire which had been in Hertfordshire unions were now administered by their own counties.

The new administration inherited much from the old, and to the recipients of relief probably seemed little different at first. The nineteenth-century workhouses, the emotive symbols of the Victorian Poor Law, passed to the new administration. By the twentieth century they had become known as 'Poor Law Institutions', but they still carried the stigma that the word 'workhouse' evokes to this day. In an attempt to improve their image, the County Council renamed them. The Royston Institution (built in 1835) became 'Royston House', that at Berkhamsted (dating from 1831) 'Nugent House' and so on. However, the character of the large, Victorian institutions, and the categories of poor housed in them remained little changed – they included the elderly, the homeless, infants and other persons in need of residential care, such as some mentally handicapped people. Under the same roof were received the 'casuals' – tramps or 'persons without a settled way of living'.

The care of children was an important responsibility inherited from the Boards of Guardians which has been undertaken by the County Council ever since. For most of the nineteenth-century babies and children in the care of the guardians were, like the young Oliver Twist, housed in the workhouse together with all the other categories of pauper. Towards the end of the century the potential harm of such a policy began to be realised and several unions, including Bishops Stortford and St Albans, began to experiment with 'cottage homes' or 'scattered homes'. Particularly when the scattered homes system was employed, as at Barnet, children were removed from the workhouse to live in relatively small numbers in ordinary houses and they attended the local elementary schools. From 1910 the government ordered that no children over three years old must live in the workhouse, and that up to the age of three they must be cared for in proper nurseries. This was the system inherited by the Area Guardians Committees, and it remained little changed until after the Second World War. Like the workhouses, the children's homes were given new names in an attempt to humanise them. The Hitchin Union Children's Home, for example, was renamed Briar Patch, and this home's successor – in new buildings and on a different site – bears the same name today. Some homes were reorganised or even closed down, because they were so unsuitable. The St Albans Union Homes at Harpenden, for example, which were renamed 'Harcourt', were inspected by a Ministry of Health inspector in 1928. She found little to praise. The staff was too small and the matron hopeless at administration, the home was overcrowded, the food was bad and insufficient, the children's underwear was in rags and the older children were responsible for dressing the younger ones who, as a result, were wearing several thick layers of woollen clothes in July. To make things even worse, at least one bed had been made with the mattress and blankets wet, and in any case the only place to wash and dry wet sheets was in the scullery where the crockery was washed up.[10] The County Council made some improvements, but the building, which consisted of two ordinary houses knocked together, was simply not suitable, and the home was closed in 1932. In general, though, the old homes continued in use and certainly the system of bringing children together in large homes remained the same.

One problem inherited from the old Boards of Guardians was the provision of accommodation for tramps, known as 'vagrants' or 'casuals', who were allowed to spend a couple of nights in the 'casual wards' of the workhouses in return for a day's work. The system was supposed to cater for those in real need, such as the unemployed travelling the country to look for work, which was not uncommon in Hertfordshire, where rural unemployment had been a major problem at least since the agricultural depression in the nineteenth century. However, as some of the workhouse casual wards were only a few miles apart, it was easy for the confirmed tramp to abuse the system. The numbers involved were not small – on one sample night in 1930 there were 688 people sleeping in casual wards in Hertfordshire, though the average for the whole year was less than 600 per night. According to a report to the County Council, the vagrants fell into one of three categories: 'Veterans who go round and round aimlessly, taking advantage of the "short circuits" created by the present distribution of the casual wards'; the genuinely out of work looking for a job – this was the smallest category; and 'men who are "out for what they can get"', who were generally criminal or potentially so.[11] The Council aimed to discourage the veterans by ensuring that no casual wards were closer than 15–20 miles apart; though as by this time it would not be difficult to find a lorry driver to give a lift to the next ward, this was obviously not a real solution to the problem. Most of the tramps were men, but there were women and even children on the circuit. One problem family consisted of a mother and father together with their four children aged six, five, three and seven months, who were dragged round the country and forced to walk long distances between each night's place of rest.[12] It was really the Second World War which put an end to the phenomenon of the rural

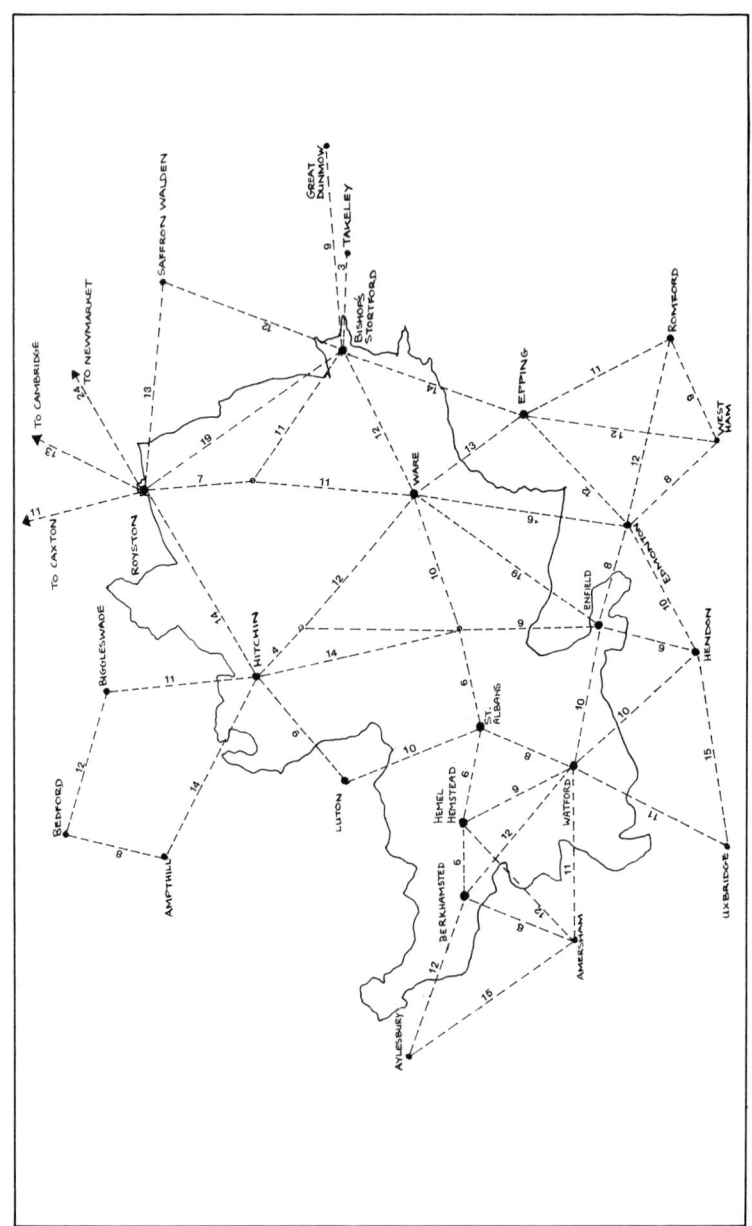

Map of the routes (distances in miles) taken by vagrants between 'casual wards' in and around Hertfordshire in 1929. When the County Council took over responsibility for providing accommodation for casuals in 1930, it aimed to discourage permanent vagrants by ensuring casual wards were at least 15–20 miles apart.

tramp and the casual wards – or at least transformed it into an urban problem. On a sample night in July 1947, only 40 admissions to a casual ward were recorded, and the wards themselves were soon to be transformed into 'reception centres' where people could stay for a short while to allow time for a decision to be made about the type of help which could best serve each individual.

Unemployment was one of the major problems of the 1920s and 1930s, but it was only for a few years in the 1930s that the payment of unemployment benefit became a direct responsibility of the County Council. A National Insurance scheme to prevent the unemployed being dependent on the Poor Law had been introduced in 1911, but even with changes and extensions to the scheme, it was not sufficient to cope with the long-term unemployment problems of the inter-war years. Many of the unemployed had to apply to the Boards of Guardians and later the County Council Guardians Committees for help, and the level of assistance given varied from area to area. In 1931, as an economy measure, the government placed restrictions on the levels of benefit which could be given to the long-term unemployed. After 26 weeks, standard unemployment benefit ceased to be paid, and application had to be made to the County Council Guardians Committee for 'transitional benefits', the amount of which was decided by the 'means test', which became notorious. Under this scheme, an applicant had to go through the demeaning process of having his household goods and potential sources of income examined, to see whether by selling items of furniture or by accepting help from a relation, he could be deemed to be able to live on less than the maximum permissible payment of 15s 3d (76p) per week, plus 8s (40p) for his wife and 2s (10p) for each child. At this time, a skilled worker earned around £3 a week, and an agricultural labourer (the lowest paid class of worker) about £1 11s (£1.55) a week, and it was considered that the minimum weekly income needed to support a man and wife and three children was 53s (£2.65). Married women could no longer apply even for unemployment benefit in their own right – however long they had paid contributions. The reduction of benefits as a result of means testing could cause considerable hardship to the unemployed and their families, and many councils (including Essex County Council) either refused outright to comply with the government's regulations, or quietly tried to avoid cutting benefits as much as the government intended. As a result, a national Unemployment Assistance Board was created in 1935 to administer unemployment benefit (and the means test) on a national basis. In Hertfordshire, the numbers of unemployed affected were tiny compared with the numbers in the depressed areas of Wales and the North-east of England, but even so, during the three years from November 1931 until December 1934 during which time the Council was responsible for administering the means test, nearly 53,000 cases were investigated (15,285 new cases plus 37,427 reviews of existing cases).[13] The largest numbers were in the Watford and Hitchin Guardians Committee Areas. Watford, where 17,549 cases were investigated (out of a total population of around 101,000) was the most populous and most industrialised area of Hertfordshire, and therefore the most susceptible to unemployment. In the Hitchin Guardians Committee Area, a rural area which had already experienced much hardship and depopulation in the nineteenth century, the proportions were much higher: 15,515 cases in an area with a population of around 42,000.

Roads and Bridges

After the First World War, private motor cars became more and more common, and the provision of good roads became ever more important, especially in Hertfordshire, through which ran the major routes north from London. Car ownership increased far more quickly in Hertfordshire than in Britain as a whole: between 1928 and 1935 the number of vehicles in the county increased by 90 per cent. With more cars came more road accidents. The Road Traffic Act of 1930 abolished speed limits for private motor vehicles, but in 1935 the 30mph speed limit was introduced in all built-up areas. Road building was encouraged by the government to provide work for the unemployed, though most of the biggest projects in Hertfordshire were not official unemployment relief schemes. The trunk roads through Hertfordshire were improved considerably during this period and many new sections were built, including the first bypasses. These included the Cambridge Arterial Road (now the A10) as far north as Turnford (an unemployment relief scheme), the Watford Bypass (A41) and the Barnet Bypass (A1), all completed in the mid 1920s. The 6½ miles of the Watford Bypass was an enormous undertaking, involving excavating half a million tons of earth and building two large bridges over railway lines and one over the River Colne. The contractor for the work was Sir Robert MacAlpine and Sons Ltd, still a familiar name today. Many of the lesser roads had never even been tarred, and there was much work on improvement and widening of roads. It is interesting in 1920 to find environmental considerations affecting the decisions of the County Council's Highways Committee, which was responsible for maintaining the roads. In that year, it was reported that the road at West Hyde (near Rickmansworth) had never been tarred because of fears of adverse effects on the watercress beds nearby (watercress growing was then an important element in the economy of the area), but the residents complained of the state of the road and requested some sort of treatment to help lay the dust from it.

Town and Country Planning

Although the County Council did not appoint a County Planning Officer until after the Second World War, it was already very concerned with the planning and conservation of the environment. Between the wars, house building boomed – over 4 million houses were built nationally – and Hertfordshire saw much of this new growth. In the southern part of the county, especially Rickmansworth and Chorleywood, there was 'Metro-land' development providing suburban homes for London commuters, though by this time there was less of this type of development than elsewhere in the home counties, since commuters had been moving into the area ever since the Metropolitan railway line reached Rickmansworth in 1887. There was even a completely new town at Welwyn Garden City which began in 1923 following the success of Letchworth which had been founded in 1903 as the first 'garden city' in the world. Both Letchworth and Welwyn Garden City grew out of the inspiration and hard work of Ebenezer Howard and were carefully planned according to the precepts laid down in *Tomorrow: A Peaceful Path to Real Reform* (1898) and *Garden Cities of Tomorrow* (1902). Each was designed to be a balanced community with industrial, commercial and residential areas and every resident had access to a garden and open space. Although the two pioneering towns were private ventures, the Hertfordshire County Council naturally took an interest in their development, and after the Second World War the concept of the garden city was to be followed on a larger scale in the government-sponsored 'new towns'.

However, unlike the garden cities, most of the new building which ate up former agricultural land in Hertfordshire was completely uncontrolled. Under the Housing and Town Planning Act 1919, the government required the larger towns to prepare town-planning schemes defining how the town should develop. In many areas such plans were ineffective or never completed, but in Hertfordshire all the local authorities in the county, urban and rural, combined under the aegis of the County Council to produce a combined plan for the whole county, in addition to their area plans. The County Council appointed a Planning Committee in 1925 and appointed a professional Planning Consultant, and in 1927 the Hertfordshire Regional Planning Report, the first to be produced for an entire county, was published. It was extremely comprehensive, covering transport, industry, occupations, public services (such as water, electricity and gas), residential development, open spaces and amenities (including advertising hoardings), and setting its aims for the county's future in the context of its past history. It is interesting that almost all the areas it identifies as causes for concern still feature today in discussions about the future of the county! The unplanned spread of bungalow growth in the Lee Valley was already a problem: people were buying up small plots of land for 'holiday homes' and building shacks which sometimes became permanent dwelling places. Even today, the after-effects of this problem have not been entirely eliminated. Already the County Council had made bye-laws to try to control the spread of advertisements over the countryside. The rapidly growing number of petrol stations along most main roads, while necessary for the motorist, were particular offenders in this respect, and the 1927 report pointed out that 'hoardings ... when erected in the wrong place can effectively destroy any pleasing effect' achieved by careful planning in town or country.[14] Almost the only change not foreseen by the plan was the growth of road transport for goods, for it proposes a greater promotion of Hertfordshire's canals for the carriage of goods, suggesting that this will relieve the railways, then the chief means of transporting goods, of some of their burden.

The planners realised how strong an influence the closeness of London is to development in Hertfordshire, and admitted that 'any new town in Hertfordshire will be, in fact, a satellite to London'.[15] It proposed 'green belts' round the larger villages, to prevent their spread into the surrounding countryside with the resulting loss of amenity and of agricultural land, and also suggested a green belt in the south of the county to prevent the spread of London. In 1934, the London County Council took up this idea and developed a comprehensive green belt scheme for London, which led to the Green Belt (London and Home Counties) Act of 1938; the foundations had been laid for the Hertfordshire County Council's acquisition after the war of large tracts of land near London to help preserve a green belt. Hertfordshire was fortunate too, that a number of large, privately owned estates such as those owned by the Marquess of Salisbury at Hatfield, the Earl of Lytton at Knebworth and Lord Desborough at Panshanger, served to preserve a green belt.

Centralisation and the Building of County Hall

For the County Council as a whole, the most important development in the period was the recognition of the need for central offices and a new meeting place for the Council, culminating in the opening of the new County Hall in 1939. Despite the expansion of services provided by the County Council, and the considerable increase in the number of employees, the different functions, represented by the offices of different County Council departments, were scattered, and there was little sense of unity. The County Clerk's offices were in Hertford, those of the County Accountant were in London and the County Surveyor was based in Hatfield. Officers from different departments even communicated by post, as if they worked for different organisations. The County Councillors themselves were remote from the Council's administration, for the full Council met alternately in Hertford and St Albans, and the committees, which developed the Council's policies, mainly met in London. Talk of centralisation began in about 1930, during the days of the depression, when the prime concern was to economise on accommodation and spending. For most departments, existing accommodation was both unsatisfactory, and quite simply too small. The County Surveyor did not have enough room in his offices at Hatfield, for example; and the Motor Taxation Department's offices were in a narrow main road in Hertford, with no parking facilities for motorists collecting car or driving licences. It was by no means certain that centralisation would necessarily be in Hertford: unlike in many counties, the county town is neither in the centre of Hertfordshire nor the largest or most accessible town. Offices in St Albans were not out of the question. However, the Clerk to the County Council was based in Hertford and was hardly likely to promote a move out of the town. As the most prominent solicitor in the area he was also in the best position to keep an eye on the local property market, so it is not surprising that in 1930 Bayley Hall in the centre of Hertford was purchased from the Trustees of Hertford Grammar School for use as additional offices. By the end of 1933 the Council had approved a plan to demolish it and build new county offices on the site. However, in 1934 Leahoe House and its extensive grounds, just outside Hertford town centre, came on the market, and the Council agreed

Top; *County Hall, Hertford, in course of construction in 1938.* Bottom; *The first County Council meeting to be held in the purpose-built Council chamber at County Hall.*

to purchase the property for £10,000. In the light of the incredible increases in land values which were to come and what would have seemed to the councillors of the 1930s the equally startling growth in the number of the Council's employees, this was one of the most fortunate decisions ever made by the Council.

The offices on the Bayley Hall site had been intended simply to house the Council's clerical staff, with Council meetings continuing to be held in the Shire Hall, Hertford and the St Albans Court House. The Central Organisation Committee had resolved in 1933 that 'it would be most convenient for the majority of the meetings of committees to be held in London.'[16] However, the offices at the Leahoe site were intended from the first to include a council chamber and committee rooms. This may perhaps have been connected with the fact that the Shire Hall in Hertford was by this time in a poor structural state. Its court room accommodation was inadequate, and suffered excessively from traffic noise; the public rooms were too small for their existing use and the Shire Hall's position made Fore Street very narrow and dangerous, so that in 1934 the possibility of demolishing it was being considered. Unfortunately for Hertford's traffic problems (though no doubt happily for admirers of the work of James Adam) the question was not pursued.

The original requirements in the public competition to design the new County Hall specified accommodation for the Clerk of the Peace, Education, Public Assistance, Motor Taxation and Weights and Measures departments, and the departments of the County Surveyor, County Architect, County Accountant, County Medical Officer and County Land Agent. The County Library headquarters were to be at Leahoe House (the nineteenth-century house at the centre of the Leahoe site) and the police headquarters were to remain at Hatfield. At that time the total clerical staff employed was under 200, but it was estimated that by 1941 there would be nearly 300. In 1936 alterations were made to the plans, slightly reducing the size of the main building, but introducing the present separate building for the Motor Taxation Department and County Library, together with the County Muniment Room and County Documents Room (the infant County Record Office), which on the original plans were in the basement of the main building. The competition, which was assessed by Robert Atkinson, FRIBA, attracted 62 entries and in October 1935 the results were announced.

The new County Hall was designed by the firm of James and Bywaters and Rowland Pierce, who were already known for their civic work, including such buildings as the City Hall at Norwich. It is of neo-Georgian design, with a copper covered cupola, a large Portland stone portico, brick arcading linking the council chamber and entrance hall to the office space and sparse, but finely detailed, decoration. It was considerably influenced by the Scandinavian style of the 1930s, and the arcading and cupola in particular are startlingly reminiscent of the Stockholm Stadshuset (Town Hall). The original furniture and fittings, particularly in the Council chamber and committee rooms, are of extremely high quality in design and craftmanship, even though the final building work had to be carried out extremely fast to enable the building to be occupied before the expected outbreak of war – otherwise, it was feared, the building might be requisitioned by the government. There were some casualties of the war, however. The planned official opening of the building by HM the Queen (now HM the Queen Mother) was abandoned on the outbreak of hostilities. The sculpted 'traffic centre pedestal' which was to have stood in the members' car park in front of the building, where the circular traffic island is now, was packed away for safety during the war and never replaced, and now stands abandoned beside Leahoe House, though plans are in hand to place it at last in its intended position. The intended tree planting was not carried out, leaving the new building in a stark concrete landscape until the 1970s, when a comprehensive tree planting programme was undertaken. The trees which are now (1988) reaching maturity have considerably softened and matured the appearance of the site. The front entrance to County Hall, impressive though it nevertheless is, was to have been even more imposing with the addition of two bronze harts sculpted by A F Hardiman. The story attached to these is a sad one. The clay models were completed, £900 of the £1,400 fee had been paid and the finished harts had been cast when the workshops of the firm carrying out the casting were destroyed by enemy action. No further steps were taken during the war, but in 1949 it was decided to go ahead with the project. Although the sculptor had died, the clay model remained in his studio and by 1951 a plaster cast had been obtained, ready for making the final casting, at a cost of £150. Unfortunately, it was felt that, having already spent over £1000 on the project, the final £1300 or so which was now needed to have the harts cast could not be afforded. The project was abandoned, the plaster casts were allowed to decay, and the county has lost a work of art. Happily, however, a new pair of harts has been commissioned to celebrate the Council's centenary in 1989.

The building of central county offices was only the most important aspect of the efforts to improve the Council's performance and build a more efficient administrative machine. The offices of the County Surveyor, County Medical Officer and County Land Agent, for example, had been separated before the building of County Hall, and may have been inadequate, but at least these Chief Officers were employed full time and were responsible only to the County Council. This was not true of the two key administrative posts of County Clerk and County Accountant. The Clerk to the County Council and Clerk of the Peace was Philip Elton Longmore. His work for the County was just one aspect of the work carried out by his firm of solicitors (which remains prominent in Hertford today). When his father, Sir Charles Elton Longmore, died in office in 1930, Philip Elton Longmore had inherited not only the firm but the clerkship; there was no question of choosing a new clerk on a competitive basis. Longmore himself spent only a few hours a week dealing with the County Council's business, but one of his clerks devoted his time to the County Council. In the nineteenth and early twentieth centuries, it was quite normal for solicitors to act as clerks to a wide variety of public and private bodies. The clerk acted under strict instructions from the body of trustees, managers, board members or councillors, and no conflict of interests was perceived. By the 1930s, however, such methods of working were completely inappropriate. The work of the

County Council, in particular, had grown enormously, so that it was not really feasible to combine the post of Clerk with other work. It was no longer possible for the Council to give detailed instructions on how to answer every letter or how to deal with every minor problem that arose and since the clerk must take more responsibility for decision-making in accordance with the Council's policy he ought also to be accountable solely to the Council. The County Council was, too, becoming active in more aspects of public life than could have been envisaged in the nineteenth century, and a clerk who was responsible to other bodies would almost certainly encounter a conflict of interests sooner or later.

P E Longmore was at least based in Hertford and was a representative of the firm which had been prominent in county affairs for many years. The situation regarding the County's finances was stranger still. The County Accountant, the chief financial officer who produced the budgets and carried out the major accounting was (and had been since 1889) the firm of W B Keen, whose offices were in London. The County Treasurer was Barclays Bank which actually looked after the County's money and there was also the County Finance Clerk, with a staff of seven by 1939, whose main responsibility was making payments by cheque (including salaries). Each of these was considered as a chief officer of the Council, completely independent from one another and responsible directly to the Council. The division of responsibilities between the County Accountant (who in some ways acted almost as an auditor) and the County Treasurer is not inexplicable, but the Finance Clerk held, as the County Accountant reported in 1939 'a post peculiar to Hertfordshire'[17], a phrase which may be interpreted in more than one way. In addition, each Chief Officer had a disbursement account and in some cases even his staff's salaries were paid from this. Not surprisingly, this was considered inefficient, and once County Hall was occupied a single department was created to deal with financial matters.

Hertfordshire at War

With the coming of war, most of the county's resources were geared towards fighting it. Building work stopped, road schemes were abandoned, the able-bodied were called up: men to join the armed forces and women to carry out essential war work. The County Council, too, concentrated its thoughts and its diminished manpower towards work essential to the war effort. Although meetings of the Council and its main committees continued, it was resolved to hold no meetings of sub-committees until after the war. In 1935, the County Council had, as required by the government, appointed an Air Raid Precautions Committee, despite the strong plea of County Alderman William Graveson (a member of the Society of Friends, and so committed to peace), that the County Council should request the government instead to take steps to ensure the abolition of warfare on the civilian population.[18] In 1937 it had appointed a full-time Air Raid Precautions Officer and by 1938 a scheme had been prepared for the organisation of Air Raid Precautions in Hertfordshire, and respirator stores (for gas-masks) had been established. By May 1939 a total of over 21,000 Air Raid

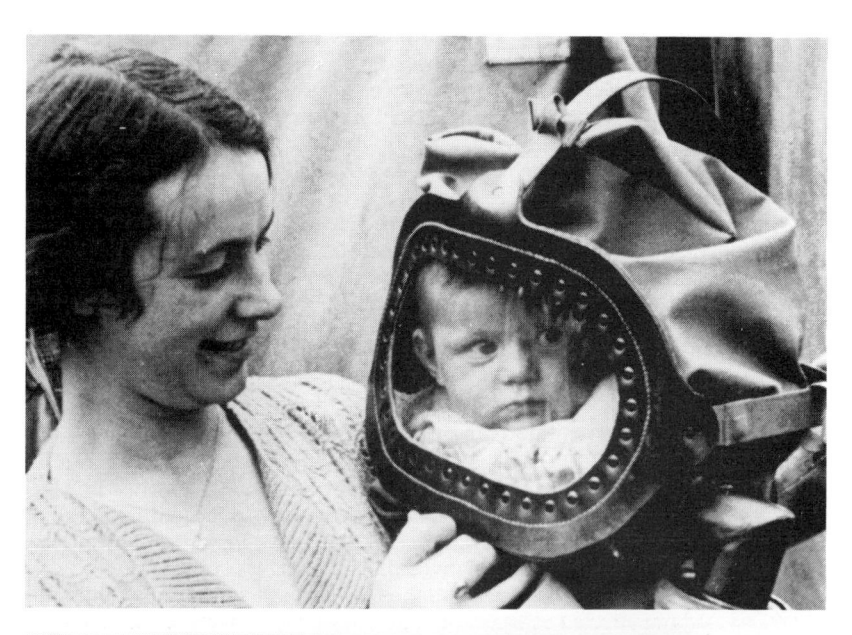

Top; *A Watford baby tries a gas mask for size during preparations for the Second World War.*
Bottom; *Evacuees from London arriving at Watford Station in 1939.*

Precautions staff had been appointed throughout the county, including 7,545 Air Raid Wardens, and 300 tons of sandbags (around 1 million bags) had been distributed to district councils, who were responsible for the detailed implementations of civil defence measures. In August a County Emergency Committee was appointed to deal with the special arrangements arising from the 'state of emergency'. One of its first actions was to purchase £550 worth of hessian (ie thousands of metres) 'for the purpose of camouflaging County Hall for Air Raid purposes',[19] presumably by wrapping the building up so it was not visible from the air. A few months later it was decided that this was, after all, no longer necessary, and the hessian was ordered to be re-sold. Hertfordshire – and the country as a whole – was deemed to be ready for war, which duly arrived on 3 September.

Hertfordshire suffered less than many counties from the effects of the war. Though close to London, it was not on the direct route to the capital followed by enemy aeroplanes, and itself contained no significant targets, so that although there was bomb damage in the county this was light compared with England as a whole. Between June 1940, when the first raids on the county took place, until the end of the war, 258 people in Hertfordshire were killed and nearly 2,000 injured, and many houses, shops and factories were damaged. The worst incident took place in Watford in June 1944, when 38 people were killed by a flying bomb and 650 houses were damaged. As an inland county, Hertfordshire was less vulnerable than maritime counties to seaborne invasion. Rationing of food and clothing affected everyone, but as a rural county Hertfordshire at least had the resources to provide much of its own food. However, the relative safety of the county, together with its proximity to London, made Hertfordshire a haven for evacuees, mainly from London, and it may be that this huge (though temporary) invasion, chiefly of children, was the most significant effect which the war had on the county. Some evacuees had arrived in 1939, but with the air raids on London of September 1940, the population of the county (then around 360,000) grew by 150,000 in just a few weeks. Many of these evacuees soon returned home, but those who stayed had to be found somewhere to sleep and eat, facilities for washing clothes and bathing, occupations for themselves and schooling for their children. To make things worse, many children were unaccompanied by their mothers. All this caused enormous problems for the County Council, the district councils and the voluntary organisations, particularly the Women's Voluntary Service (now the Women's Royal Voluntary Service), who not only had to deal with the purely administrative problems, but also with the social problems which arose. Many 'horror stories' have been reported of children from the London slums shocking their country hosts with their poverty and habits, but as a progress report to the County Council's Education Committee explained in 1941, even in the best of circumstances, welcoming evacuees was far from straightforward:

> To the majority of housewives in the reception areas, 'the war' means the loss of privacy; strangers in the kitchen; other people's children – whose habits invariably suffer by comparison with their own – constantly in the way. There has been much wishful thinking and a deal of nonsense

written about 'hostesses' and 'guests'. The relationship of householder to evacuee is rarely explicable in such terms ... [Successful evacuation] cannot be obtained by simply leaving people to adapt themselves to the social upheaval which has in fact taken place ... The physical transference of people from one area to another is child's play compared with the problem of getting strangers to live together in strange homes under war conditions and on the solution of this problem much depends.[20]

The sort of measures adopted to try to solve the problems included communal laundry and bathing facilities, nurseries for young children, community and social clubs and classes to keep adult evacuees out of the way of their 'hosts' as much as possible. 'Communal feeding centres' were established for evacuee children. These were generally in schools and the children often grew in the school gardens the vegetables they ate. Children also helped even more directly with the war effort. In handicraft classes they made for the Red Cross such useful objects as ward screens for hospitals, crutches, splints and bedside lamps. In the period from November 1940 to February 1941, one school was reported to have made 148 Aldous [ie Aldis] Lamp Stowage Boxes; 2508 Electric Plug Chains; 1,497 Mirror Reflector Tubes and many other such items for the war effort.[21]

It was probably the education of the evacuee children, many of whom arrived in organised groups, together with the disruption caused to the education of Hertfordshire children, which caused the greatest problems. In 1939, Hertfordshire's elementary schools had just over 46,000 children on roll. By January 1940, the schools had to cope with an additional 14,000 children who came to the county as evacuees. In July 1940 another 8,000 arrived (from Hastings and Eastbourne) and by January 1941 there were 25,000 evacuee schoolchildren in the county. Numbers of evacuees fell as the war progressed, but they remained a significant proportion of the school population. Most of these children came with their schools, so in effect whole 'foreign' schools (generally with some of their teachers) were billeted on Hertfordshire schools. Various ways were developed of meeting the demand for teaching space. At first, schools often ran a 'double shift' system with the host school using the premises in the morning or afternoon only and the guest school taking the other shift. Sometimes the shifts would consist of three days a week each. However, the policy of the Education Department was that wherever possible, normal school hours would be maintained, and even by the end of November 1939, 164 halls had been rented and 85 per cent of the schools in affected areas of the county were running normal hours. In general, the evacuated schools retained their own identity and teachers, but in some cases teachers were pooled, effectively creating new schools. In Aldbury, for example, in 1939 there were 163 evacuated children from three schools, each with their own head teachers. The existing village school had 77 children on roll. All the children were grouped into two shifts of about 120 each, each shift spending half its time in the school and half in the village hall. As well as making the best use of the available premises, this arrangement enabled some teachers to return to teach in London.

As many mothers were engaged in various kinds of war work, the Education Department developed schemes to look after both pre-school and school-age children while their mothers were at work. By November 1942, 35 'wartime nurseries' had been established in the county, with accommodation for 1,568 children; and there were sixteen play centres which looked after school-age children until 6.30pm.

As well as children still at school, the county also had responsibility for those who had left school but were not yet old enough to join the armed forces. Counties were ordered by the government to formulate a policy to meet the needs of youths aged 14–18 'to prevent the recurrence during this war of the social problems which arose in the last'[22] as a result of the disorganisation of family life and the disruption of parental discipline, exacerbated by the blackout. Youth organisations such as the Scouts and Guides were encouraged and youth clubs were set up. In 1942 the government introduced compulsory registration for everyone aged between 16 and 18, and county councils had to make attempts to persuade those who were not continuing their education to become actively involved in a youth organisation. Cuffley Camp, where thousands of Hertfordshire schoolchildren have enjoyed a week or two's education outdoors, was a wartime product, opened in May 1943 originally for use by youth groups and as a holiday camp for young war workers. The use by schools, for which it has become known, began as a rather tentative experiment.

At the end of the First World War, the County Council had been a low profile and essentially amateur organisation, with part-time officers, easy-going (though often dedicated) councillors and scattered offices. By the end of the Second World War it had celebrated its half-century, established for itself a permanent meeting place and administrative centre, become a hard working and professional organisation, and had demonstrated its increasing importance to the people of Hertfordshire.

4
Confidence and Expansion 1945–1974

The effects of the war on the people of Britain did not cease with the arrival of peace in 1945. Food and clothes were still rationed, and in 1947 even bread and potatoes, freely available during the war, were rationed for the first time. In 1947, too, following the hard winter of 1946/47, there was a severe shortage of fuel. Food rationing lasted until 1954, and the last National Service recruit was conscripted as late as November 1960. However, the mood of the post-war era was optimistic, and set the tone for the decades to come. Local government, in Hertfordshire as elsewhere, entered a new phase of growth and major change. By the late 1950s, the age of austerity was giving way to the age of prosperity, with Harold Macmillan as Prime Minister assuring the British public that 'You've never had it so good'. Television made its appearance in most homes – already in 1952 the Hertfordshire Medical Officer of Health was concerned that children's health was suffering because of late nights and lack of exercise caused by watching television.[1] In 1958 the country's first motorway (the M6 Preston Bypass) was opened, followed in 1959 by the Hertfordshire section of the M1, and the number of private cars was rising sharply. The 1960s were the affluent age of pop culture and the permissive society. Local government was spending more and more, but by the end of the decade it was becoming obvious that the money needed to support such expansion would not last for ever. In 1966 there was a major national economic crisis, followed by a devaluation of sterling in 1967. The 1970s saw the beginnings of mounting inflation and in 1973 came the first oil crisis. Unemployment began to rise, so that in 1975 over 1 million people in Britain were without jobs for the first time since the war, though as always Hertfordshire in its wealthy home counties position was one of the least affected areas of Britain.

The enormous changes in the post-war period were most evident in the new services the County Council was called upon by central government to provide. For the first time, there was a county-wide Fire Service, and the Hertfordshire Police now served the whole of the county outside the Metropolitan Police District; a new Town and Country Planning Department was set up; welfare responsibilities underwent great changes, though with the establishment of the National Health Service, the County Council was no longer responsible for running hospitals. Education, and particularly secondary education, became an ever more important area of concern and with new schools erected all over the county, Hertfordshire County Council was stamping its mark on the physical environment too. The County Council – and district councils as well – now affected the lives of every man, woman and child in Hertfordshire more deeply than ever before. A child could now attend a county school, in a building designed by the County Architect's department, and have regular health inspections by County Council medical staff either in school, or in a new Council health centre. On leaving school he or she could find work with the help of the Council's careers service or go on to higher education with the aid of a County Council grant. Adults could carry on their education at a county college and use the services of the County Library. Most health services were provided by central government, and council housing by district councils, but it was the County Council which provided health centres, and housing for homeless families, and homes for children, the elderly and the disabled. Ambulance and fire services were provided by the county, and the roads built and maintained by the County Council (including the new motorways, built on behalf of the government) were patrolled by the Hertfordshire Police. Finally, the county's planning responsibilities affected all aspects of the environment, from the use of advertising placards in country districts, to the siting of new industrial areas. Though many people remained unsure *which* council was providing all these services, most were aware that the local authorities had a profound impact on their lives.

Partly because of the increasingly uncertain economic situation, there was growing interference in local government affairs by the central government of the day. Although under existing legislation the powers of central government to compel local authorities to act in a particular way were limited, in practice it was possible by means of ministerial advice and persuasion to guide most authorities towards carrying out official policy. In 1965, for example, the famous circular 10/65 was issued, instructing education authorities to prepare plans for all-ability secondary education, an instruction which all but a handful of authorities obeyed. In 1965, too, the reorganisation of local government in London came into effect, abolishing the London and Middlesex County Councils and creating the Greater London Council and the 32 London Boroughs. At the same time, the Barnet and East Barnet Urban Districts were transferred from Hertfordshire to the new London Borough of Barnet, while Potters Bar Urban District (formerly in Middlesex) came into Hertfordshire. Central influence on local authorities culminated in the Local Government Act of 1972 which, with effect from 1974, changed the local government map of England and Wales.

Those who worked in Hertfordshire during this period recall it as one of intense activity and commitment to meet the challenges of the fastest growing county population in the country: to provide the colleges, schools, libraries and many other facilities families would need; and to develop new concepts and standards of service in fields which had inevitably been so neglected during the war and even before. Hertfordshire not only attracted able senior officers with national reputations, such as John Newsom, Sidney Broad, Charles Aslin, Stirrat Johnson-Marshall, Ernest Doubleday, Lorna Paulin and Sylvia Watson. Young professionals in the fields of education, architecture and planning also flocked to the county to gain experience before going on to senior appointments with other authorities throughout the country.

Local Politics

It was, perhaps, as a result of the new nationwide importance of local government, and because of the national government's new-found interest in it, that national issues and national politics began to be a factor in local government elections, and the results of the elections became increasingly used as indicators of national voting patterns. Before the war, local government elections, at least in Hertfordshire, had generally been uncontroversial affairs, fought (if contested at all) on local issues. Councillors tended to be volunteers with time to spare to serve their county and they were frequently elected unopposed. There were no local government or national elections during the war, so the County Council elections of 1946 were the first for twelve years and the first to be fought seriously by the Labour Party in Hertfordshire. Sixty-one of the 66 seats (88 seats including the County Aldermen) were contested and the Labour Party – following their victory in the general election the previous year – won 19 seats. Even so, the Conservatives still did not consider themselves as a party group on the Council and did not fight the Hertfordshire elections as a group until the following election in 1949.

County council and district council elections, held every three years, did not normally coincide with general elections, and so their results came to be examined eagerly as an indication of national voting patterns; it was increasingly assumed that people would vote on party lines. In Hertfordshire, the Conservatives remained in the majority throughout this period, for most of those County Councillors who described themselves as 'independent' members still allied themselves to the Conservative group, giving it a permanent majority. However, the Labour group varied in size from election to election, peaking at 30 members in 1964: significantly, this was also the year of the general election which brought a Labour Government back to power under Harold Wilson.

Civil Defence

Once the war had ended, it was no longer an immediate necessity to continue arrangements for protecting the civilian population from the effects of enemy action, but the government was unwilling to dispense with the organisation and expertise which the war had necessitated. In 1948, under the Civil Defence Act, county councils became responsible for organising a Civil Defence Corps, mainly consisting of volunteers. By 1952 there were 3,900 members of the corps in Hertfordshire, and the county aimed to provide a Civil Defence Training Centre in every town; eventually there were 25 centres in the county where volunteers could be trained. By 1962, the corps had over 7,000 members in Hertfordshire, but in that year the number was halved when the government laid down much stricter control over membership, in order to achieve a small but highly trained band of volunteers. In 1967 the government made enormous cuts in defence spending generally and civil defence was one of the areas in which economies were made. The Civil Defence Corps was disbanded and the county's duties were restricted to preparing plans for arrangements to be made in the event of war, including training staff sufficiently to ensure local government could be carried on in wartime. The County Council, however, considered that these minimum requirements were not sufficient to protect the population of Hertfordshire, and voted money from the rates (totalling more than the government grant) towards civil defence. The county's civil defence staff was cut drastically (from 45 people to 7), but more training was given to local authority staff than the required minimum, and although the corps was disbanded, many former members continued to meet and train at their own expense, with the encouragement of the County Council.

Although the training of the Civil Defence Corps would have enabled them to assist in the event of peacetime as well as wartime emergencies, the emphasis of the Civil Defence Department's work was firmly on planning for the event of war, and specifically the threat of nuclear war. The aims of the detailed Hertfordshire County Council war plan produced in 1968 were succinctly expressed: 'co-ordinating the resources available within the County to ensure the survival of as many people as possible after a nuclear attack[2] and the measures adopted in the plan included the provision of fall-out shelters, burial of the dead, mass-feeding, accommodation for the homeless and prevention of epidemics. It is true that in 1968 the much-reduced Civil Defence Department was given responsibility for road safety training, but this was mainly a matter of administrative convenience, and it was not until 1973 that plans were drawn up for coping with peacetime emergencies such as major air crashes or natural disasters like fire or flood.

Fire and Ambulance Service

The most important of the new services for which the County Council became responsible after the war was the Fire Service. From at least the eighteenth century, most parishes had had their fire engine, often stored in the parish church, and in many places this arrangement continued until the First World War, but during the nineteenth century voluntary fire brigades had been set up, and some district councils began to maintain their own fire brigades. During the Second World War it was realised that although local fire brigades might be efficient in providing fire protection in peacetime, a co-ordinated approach to the emergency services was essential in wartime. The National Fire Service was created in 1941 to ensure a speedy response both to ordinary fires and to those caused by incendiary bombs and other incidents of enemy action. After the war, the National Fire Service organisation was used as the foundation of the new county brigades created under the Fire Services Act 1947, and the Hertfordshire Fire Brigade came into being on 1 April 1948.

When the Hertfordshire Fire Brigade took over from the National Fire Service, the first Chief Fire Officer, Geoffrey Blackstone, aimed to make the new service as efficient and cheap as possible without reducing the standards of protection. He sought to reduce the number of personnel inherited from the NFS, proposing a reduction from 174 to 138 personnel and so cutting the annual wages bill to £57,000 – a tiny sum when compared with today's wage bill of around £9 million a year (in fact, the number of firemen, both full and part-time, grew during the Hertfordshire Fire Brigade's first few years). Another way of improving efficiency was to close some fire stations, such as that at Bushey, which was covered by Watford Fire Station, and those in the villages of Benington and Walkern, which could be covered from Stevenage. Over the years, other stations were built or replaced; the old Watford station, built at the turn of the century, closed in 1961, when it was replaced by a brand-new station costing £79,000, while the Hitchin station (costing just £711 when it was built in 1904) was replaced in 1968.

The first headquarters of the Hertfordshire Fire Brigade was at Leahoe House at County Hall in Hertford. As the establishment grew to keep pace with the ever-increasing workload, Leahoe was no longer large enough, and in April 1964, the headquarters was transferred to the new purpose-built fire station and headquarters building in London Road, Hertford. The official opening of the new building by the Lord Lieutenant of Hertfordshire on 19 September 1964 was the occasion for the first review and display by the Fire and Ambulance Brigades since 1949, with headquarters staff dressed in uniforms from the 1880s, and demonstrations of fire-fighting techniques from the past alongside the most up-to-date methods.

Before the war, ambulance services had been run by most district councils in conjunction with local hospitals, but on the outbreak of war they became part of the County Civil Defence service. At the end of the war, when the civil defence organisations were wound up, the Hertfordshire district councils once again took responsibility – though with ambulances provided by the County Council – but in July 1948 the County Council took full responsibility for Hertfordshire's ambulance service. The fire and ambulance services were run as a joint brigade until April 1974 when responsibility for the ambulance service passed to the Area Health Authorities. In 1949 the service had 52 ambulances, together with 16 cars for patients who did not need to lie down. By the time the County Council handed over responsibility for the service, there were actually fewer ambulances (45), but these were fully used and were supplemented by 64 other vehicles. However, the number of patients carried increased dramatically: in 1949 there were fewer than 90,000 calls, but during 1972, nearly 400,000 patients were carried, and the vehicles travelled nearly 3 million miles.

During the war, voluntary drivers for organisations like the Red Cross, the St John's Ambulance Association and the Women's Voluntary Service had helped the official ambulance service by taking patients to and from hospitals in their own cars, and the ambulance service continued to accept this help once the war finished. In the 1950s there was already a growing preference for treating people as out-patients rather than keeping them in hospital for extended periods, and this was one reason for retaining the volunteer car service. However, it was considered preferable to carry patients in ambulances wherever possible, and

Top; *Members of the Hertfordshire Fire Brigade from Rickmansworth in 1951, with a former National Fire Service water tender transferred to the County Fire Brigade on its formation in 1948.* Bottom; *Radio operator on duty at Police Headquarters, Hatfield, in 1954. The Hertfordshire Constabulary was the first force in the world to operate centrally-controlled two-way radio in police vehicles.*

efforts were made to reduce the numbers carried by car. Even so, voluntary transport continued to be used until 1974.

Ambulances are most visible when rushing to meet emergency calls to accidents or cases of sudden illness. Certainly such emergencies produce incidents to demonstrate the skill and dedication of members of the service, such as happened on a dark February morning in 1967. An ambulance driver was on the carriageway of the M1 motorway treating a driver injured in a road accident. Another car broke through the bollards placed by the police, knocked down the ambulance man, ran over the man whose broken knee he was treating, crashed into the already damaged car and injured two further people. Despite his own injuries, the ambulance man continued to treat all the other casualties before reporting sick himself.[3] However, such cases of heroism form only a small part of the service's work: in 1972 fewer than 5 per cent of calls were to cases of sudden illness or accident. The essential work remained the conveyance of patients to and from hospital.

Police

For the police force, the years following the Second World War saw another period of reform and renewal. Efforts were made to improve the force's image, the standing of the profession and the quality of recruits: of the 265 men accepted into the force between 1955 and 1959, only 52 had GCE O levels, and only one had A levels. A proper cadet training system was started with both academic and practical training, though women cadets were not accepted until the 1960s. The size of the establishment (ie the theoretical strength of the force) was increased considerably in the 1960s and 1970s, reflecting the increase in crime in those years, but recruitment was a great problem; in 1965 there were 465 vacancies out of a total theoretical establishment of 1,339. Recruitment improved in the 1970s, but until 1981 the force remained significantly below its authorised strength.

The most important developments for the efficiency of the force came in the field of communications. After the Second World War, police pillars with telephones connected to the police station were introduced (the St Albans City Police began the system in the 1930s), partly for the use of the constable on his beat, and partly for the use of members of the public, who were, however, reluctant to use them. Much more significant, though, was the introduction of radio. Police vehicles carried radio from 1947 – the Hertfordshire force was the first in the world to operate two-way radio in police vehicles. From the mid-1960s, personal pocket radios were used by each man on the beat; the pilot scheme began in Stevenage in November 1965. Today, radio communication is of course an essential tool of the police force.

Traffic patrols could be said to have originated in the cycle corps known as the 'scorchers' set up in 1899, one of whose functions was to catch speeding (pedal) cyclists, but they achieved their real significance after the opening of the M1 motorway in 1959. The Hertfordshire Police also became responsible for manning the emergency service telephones on the ever-increasing network of motorways. The increase in the number of motor vehicles led to traffic congestion and the imposition of parking restrictions so although there was a certain amount of opposition both within and outside the force, traffic wardens were introduced in the 1960s. The first experimental scheme began in St Albans on 1 April 1964.

The use of dogs is a routine aspect of police work today, but a permanent unit was not established in Hertfordshire until 1951. That first unit consisted of just three dogs and their handlers, who were responsible for a normal beat as well as for their special duties with the dogs. The following year, one of the dogs, 'Rajah' was shot and wounded by a suspect whom he had tracked from the scene of a burglary in Brookmans Park; the first time a British police dog had been injured in this way. An important precedent was set when the offender was found guilty of using a firearm with intent to resist arrest even though it was the dog, not the handler who was attacked. By 1965 there were 7 teams, and by 1986, the dog unit consisted of 1 inspector, 2 sergeants and 22 constables, and included 2 dogs whose sole job was the detection of explosive devices.

Before the war, the 'village bobby' known to everyone was the norm, but with the introduction of anonymous car patrols, public relations worsened considerably, and since then various approaches have been tried to improve the quality of policing. In the 1960s, the 'neighbourhood beat' was introduced, beginning in Hemel Hempstead in 1962. The new towns like Hemel Hempstead were planned in terms of separate neighbourhoods, intended to provide residents with a local identity and local facilities at a more accessible level than that of the whole town. Each neighbourhood was given its own policeman, whose job was to identify himself with the community and with local organisations and to make himself known to the residents. This was very different from the previous system, where a large area was policed by a large group of police who changed shift by shift. The neighbourhood beat system was soon introduced in other urban areas, such as Watford, and in country areas a similar system was introduced in 1967. At the same time, 'unit policing' was introduced, which grouped neighbourhoods into units, each with a patrol car.

Highways

The work of the County Surveyor's Department continued to develop after the war as the amount of traffic on Hertfordshire's roads grew and grew. In 1950 there were around 74,000 vehicles in Hertfordshire; by 1960 there were nearly 170,000 and by 1970 over 300,000 – a growth of over 400 per cent in just twenty years. Amongst other problems, all these vehicles caused increasing congestion in the towns, and several bypasses were built to relieve this pressure. The demands of the inhabitants of Markyate for a bypass for the A5 was one of the first mass protests of its kind, with villagers blocking the traffic and attracting nation-wide sympathetic publicity. The Markyate Bypass was completed in

1957, and others such as London Colney (1959) and Stevenage, which became part of the A1(M) (1962) followed soon after.

The department's most important achievement, though, was the building of Britain's first major motorway. Responsibility for the design and building of the Hertfordshire section of the M1/M10 was delegated from central government. Plans for this section of road – referred to right up to the time of opening simply as the 'St Albans Bypass' – had been considered before the war to relieve the traffic problems of St Albans, but as a trunk road it was to be of much wider significance. The first section of the road (the stretch between the present junctions 7 and 10, together with the present M10 from Park Street to the M1) opened on 2 November 1959 and the second section (M1 junctions 5 to 7) in December 1959. The volume of traffic through St Albans was indeed reduced by 11,800 vehicles per day, but the road's function as a bypass for the city was overshadowed by its increasing importance as a trunk road – less than a year after its completion the short section of the road between junctions 7 and 8 was carrying an average of 21,600 vehicles per day. This was considered heavy at the time, but today the same section carries over seven times as many vehicles (155,300). Despite what was for the 1950s a huge volume of traffic, the County Council was pleased to learn that soon after its opening, the accident rate was well below average for trunk roads. On the other hand 'the number and rate of breakdowns on the motorway has far exceeded anything ever before experienced on any Trunk Road'[4]: the vehicles of the time were simply not designed to cope with travelling for prolonged periods at such high speeds.

Construction work on the M1/M10 motorway, May 1959.

Town and Country Planning

Although some work had been done in the 1930s to regulate building and to develop the environment in a controlled way, the Town and County Planning Act of 1947 gave county councils major new responsibilities, and in 1947 a County Planning Officer, E H Doubleday, was appointed for Hertfordshire, and the Planning Department was created. From the start, its work was carried out in the context of the 'new towns'.

The creation of new towns to relieve the weight of population from London and the other big cities had been suggested by Ebenezer Howard and others many years before, but it was not until the publication of Sir Patrick Abercrombie's Greater London Plan in 1944 and the New Towns Act of 1946 that they actually came into existence. Four of the original eleven English new towns were in Hertfordshire including Stevenage, which in 1946 became the first to be designated a new town. All four – Stevenage, Hemel Hempstead, Welwyn Garden City and Hatfield – were based on existing towns, but they were essentially new settlements of a size hitherto almost unknown in the county. Although the County Planning Department was not directly involved in the design of the towns, there was consultation between the county planners and those of the new towns; G A Jellicoe who prepared the Master Plan for Hemel Hempstead had actually served as the county's planning consultant until the Planning Department was created. The County Council as a whole also played a major role in providing schools, health centres and other facilities for the predominantly young residents of the new towns.

By the 1960s, one in five of Hertfordshire residents lived in one or other of the four new towns, and the presence of the new towns influenced planning decisions more than any other single factor, and completely changed the character of the county. Although many regretted the building of the new towns, and proposals for their expansion still arouse strong feeling, they did enable large and necessary post-war development to be provided without destroying the character of most of the county and its communities. Some would claim Hertfordshire – if not all of its individual towns – as a vindication of post-war town planning.

Largely because of the new towns, together with the London County Council estates built in Oxhey and Borehamwood, and because of the continuing attraction the county offered to commuters working in London, the population of Hertfordshire rose enormously in the post-war years. By the 1960s, it was double what it had been in 1931, and nearly four times the size it had been when the County Council was created in 1889. It was in this context of a rapidly increasing population that the new department had to work.

The Planning Department's first duty was to carry out a survey of the county and to compile a Development Plan for Hertfordshire, which had to be approved by the Minister of Town and Country Planning, and to which future development would have to conform. The plan for Hertfordshire, finally approved in 1953, identified a number of areas of concern. In the towns there was an urgent need for more housing, which should be situated away from industrial areas and yet close to shopping facilities. Certain areas were specifically designated for residential development, and others for industry or commerce. More and better roads, and particularly car parks had to be planned, and had to be put where they were most needed. In the countryside, many areas were designated as open space, with green belts around many towns in addition to the great green belt around London. Interestingly in view of current concerns, the most difficult problem of all highlighted in the development plan was said to be the control of gravel working. It was acknowledged that Hertfordshire's only important mineral resource should be exploited, but this risked doing enormous harm to the environment.

The other main duty of the new department was to examine applications for all types of development in the county, from new housing and industrial estates down to house extensions and garages. During its first year alone, 5,612 applications were received, including 181 for new estates, 1,062 for 'minor additions' to houses and 1,274 for garages or sheds. The number of applications received grew considerably, so that in the mid-1960s over 10,000 applications were dealt with each year. Not surprisingly, perhaps, the greatest increase was in applications for residential development.

The metropolitan green belt had been planned in the 1930s as a ring of open space around London, and the Hertfordshire County Council played a major part in preserving the green belt. It had purchased the first of its green belt estates, the High Canons estate at Shenley, in 1937 – this was actually before the passing of the Green Belt (London and Home Counties) Act in 1938 confirmed that it was lawful for county councils to buy land in order to preserve it perpetually as open space. After the war, further green belt estates were purchased, bringing the total acreage of green belt land held to around 4,000 acres. Most of this land was concentrated in four estates, High Canons, the Wall Hall estate at Aldenham, Dyrham Park (in Ridge and South Mimms) and Wrotham Park (South Mimms).

Welfare Services

After the war, the government pursued a wide-ranging policy of social and economic reform which affected health, welfare services and education as well as planning, housing and industry. When the old Poor Law was finally abolished in 1948, and the National Health Service was created, hospitals and other aspects of health care were no longer run by the county councils. Certain former Poor Law institutions, mainly those already used as hospitals, such as Haymeads Hospital, Bishops Stortford (now part of the Herts and Essex Hospital) and Chalkdell, Hitchin (now the Hitchin Hospital) were transferred to the new Regional Hospital Boards. This specialisation of function, the post-war feeling that health and welfare services were best organised by type rather than by geographical area, was reflected within the County Council's organisation, in Hertfordshire as elsewhere. From 1948, when Guardians Committees were wound up, until the 1960s, health and welfare services were organised for the whole county by category. Three new committees and three corresponding departments reflected this change: the Committee for the Care of Children and the Health and Welfare Committees; and the Children's Department (created in 1950, before which it was part of the Education Department) and the Health and Welfare Departments. In 1965 the Health and Welfare departments combined, and in 1971 the Social Services Department was created, bringing together the care of children, the homeless, the elderly and others in need of assistance. Although this move was welcomed in Hertfordshire, it is an example of central government policy affecting local authorities, for the changes were brought about by Act of Parliament, not by local initiative. The county was divided into seven social services divisions, based on those already used by the Children's Department, reflecting the modern preference for integrated care within the community rather than by type of need. Separate institutions have been maintained for the elderly, for the mentally ill and for those children who cannot be fostered, but it is interesting to reflect that in some ways the pendulum has swung back towards the early twentieth century ideal of treating people in the area in which they live, with an organisation and an office close to their homes rather than in a remote part of the county. People remain in their own homes if possible, with institutionalisation as a last resort – not very different from the aims of the Boards of Guardians and Area Guardians Committees. The old workhouses themselves survived until recently as residential care institutions, quite apart from those still in use by the National Health Service as hospitals. Western House in Ware, the vast Poor Law institution built in 1840 to house 300 'inmates', closed as a home for the elderly only in 1983. As late as 1955 it was still being used for vagrants as well – a trace of the old system of putting all the needy in the workhouse. Similarly, Heath Lodge (previously known as Royston House), the former Royston Union Workhouse, housed vagrants until 1962, together with the elderly until 1964 and the homeless until 1970.

Under the National Assistance Act of 1948, the County Council was required to provide accommodation for the elderly and infirm and for others unable to look after themselves. The largest category of those who needed accommodation was the elderly. In some cases, elderly people were housed in National Health Service hospitals, but more often they were accommodated in County Council homes. Some of these (such as Western House, Ware, or Waverley Lodge, St Albans) were the old Poor Law institutions, but accommodation on a more domestic scale was provided in smaller purpose built or specially adapted homes such as Whitney Wood, Stevenage, opened in 1952 or Heath House, Bushey, built in 1961.

Accommodation for evicted and otherwise homeless families also continued to be provided in the old workhouses after 1948, but from the mid-1950s such families were generally accommodated in houses provided by the district councils or in surplus County Council premises such as police houses. The county also ran hostels at Heath Lodge in Royston and at a former Land Army hostel at Northchurch, Berkhamsted. Northchurch Hostel was replaced by the purpose-built Chilterns in 1968, and Heath Lodge by Ridgeway in 1970. By the 1960s at least these hostels were used mainly for 'problem' families who were not capable of being rehoused immediately in normal accommodation, and the new premises were called 'family centres' rather than 'hostels' in order to emphasise their more positive role.

From the 1960s, the County Council also became more actively involved in mental health care, particularly under the provisions of the Mental Health Act 1959 which sought to reduce the institutional care of the mentally ill and mentally handicapped. In 1963, for example, Beaconsfield was opened at St Albans as a hostel for employable mentally handicapped men, and in 1967 Roundwood, also in St Albans, for severely mentally handicapped adults. Provision was also made for the care of the mentally ill, with unstaffed hostels such as Granville Road, Watford, opened in 1968, or Jessup Road, Stevenage, opened in 1967.

Children

In 1948 the care of children became the responsibility of the new Children's Committee and Children's Department. The first Children's Officer, Sylvia Watson was appointed from the Education Department. She was the first woman to be appointed a Chief Officer of the County Council (Mary Austin had been appointed County Librarian earlier in 1948, but she worked within the Education Department). Several of the residential nurseries which accommodated the youngest children were still in the former workhouses, and where the institution passed to the National Health Service, the nurseries had perforce to be closed. But in any case, the importance was now being seen of allowing children in care to experience as far as possible a normal family life. The larger children's homes were closed, such as Ashby Road, Watford, renamed 'Merryfield', which had housed over 80 children in the 1930s, and which was closed in December 1955, or Cattsdells, Hemel Hempstead, closed in June 1955. The new order was typified by the four small 'family group homes' opened in 1962 in the new town of Hemel Hempstead, each for just eight or nine children. From 1970, as a result of the Children and Young Persons Act 1969 the children's homes all became known as 'community homes'. Amongst other provisions the Act abolished the approved schools and remand homes, so Pishiobury and Danesbury Approved Schools which were run by the County Council became community homes like other accommodation for children. The concept of punishment in a special institution was officially abolished, and more emphasis was placed on the work of the new observation and assessment centres, like those at Bushey and Stevenage, to assess the type of care appropriate for each child.

From at least the 1940s Children's Department workers recognised the importance of giving as many children as possible the chance of a normal family life. One way of doing this was through adoption or fostering. In 1948 nearly 500 children in the care of the County Council lived in homes, and fewer than 200 were in foster homes. Twenty years later, in 1968, only 270 lived in homes and over 550 in foster homes. By 1986, another twenty years on, 137 children lived in community homes, while 468 were fostered. Not only did the number of children in care go down, but the proportions of those in care compared with those fostered had reversed (though the change did not take place as steadily as these sample figures may suggest). After the Adoption Act 1958, children were placed directly for adoption as well as for fostering. The Hertfordshire County Council became and remains the largest adoption agency in the country, and is also responsible for monitoring and advising on all applications for adoptions.

Rather than taking children at risk into care at all, much time and effort was spent on trying to keep them in their own families. Although some work in this area was already being done, it became a much more important aspect of the work of the Children's Department and later of the Social Services Department following the passing of the Children and Young Persons Act 1963, which made it a duty for councils to provide advice and assistance to families in order to diminish the need to take children into care or bring them before the courts. Only two years after the Act came into force, the department was already supervising nearly three times as many children living with their parents as separated from them.

Schools

The major changes affecting education in the post-war period were a result of the Education Act of 1944 (the Butler Act) which made compulsory implementation of many of the ideas which had been put forward in the 1926 Hadow report. The most far-reaching provisions were the change of school at the age of eleven and the division of secondary education – which was to be free at all maintained secondary schools – into grammar, technical and modern schools. The school leaving age was raised to fifteen (with effect from 1947), and it was intended that it should soon be raised to sixteen. The Act would also have required everyone under the age of eighteen who was not in full-time education to attend a county college one day a week. This was never fully brought into force, though it did lead to an increase in day release study and to the building of some County Colleges. Until 1944, half the children in Hertfordshire County Grammar schools had won free education by passing the County Special Place Examination, but the remainder paid fees for their schooling. Now secondary education at all levels became free for everyone. Examinations (the 'eleven plus') still determined who received a grammar school education, though the original plan, never to be fulfilled, was that this should be an interim measure, only to be used until there were enough schools of all types for everyone to receive the education of their choice.

In Hertfordshire, the work of reorganisation was not as great as it might have been, with 'Hadow reorganisation' already well under way before the war – but it was a large enough task that Sir John Newsom had to carry out as County Education Officer. In 1944, Hertfordshire had nearly 51,000 children in elementary schools, nearly 9 per cent of whom were of secondary school age. In Bishops Stortford, to take just one area, there were in 1944 eight elementary schools. Four of these took children from the ages of 5 to 14; three from 7 to 14 and one from 5 to 7. A new secondary modern school had to be built, and all the elementary schools had to be reorganised as junior mixed or junior mixed and infants schools. As well as the new range of secondary schools now required, the school population was growing rapidly, increasing by 70 per cent in the decade from 1944 to 1954. Many school buildings needed replacing because they had been damaged in the war, or simply because they were so old. The new County Architect's Department had to develop pioneering new methods of working in order to provide the buildings required (see page 75).

Some wartime developments made a long-term impact on education: the provision of school meals, for example, owes much to the war. Local Education Authorities had been allowed to provide meals for undernourished schoolchildren from 1906, and at some Hertfordshire schools, meals had indeed been provided, either by the County Council or by voluntary efforts. The service had been very limited, and in 1939 just 958 Hertfordshire children had a midday meal at school. During the war, the number rose enormously: it was convenient to feed evacuees of all ages communally at school, and by 1944, 23,576 school meals were served each day. The 1944 Education Act made compulsory the provision both of school meals and milk, and by 1957, 67,000 meals were served daily.

Examinations have always been a feature of school life: school exemption examinations; scholarship examinations; the 'eleven plus'. Before the Second World War it was mainly the more academically minded children who sat external examinations. Since the war, 'paper qualifications' have become ever more important, and efforts have been made to give every child the chance to demonstrate his or her level of achievement to prospective employers. In 1951, the General Certificate of Education (O levels) replaced the old School Certificate throughout the country. Instead of having to pass examinations in a whole range of subjects at a time, a qualification could be gained in just one or two subjects. The new examination had no age limit, so both 'late developers' and adults also had the chance to sit the new exams. However, the new examinations were no use to the least academic children – typically those in the secondary modern schools whose skills tended to be practical ones. It was to enable these children to obtain qualifications that Hertfordshire pioneered the award of area certificates. The syllabus for each subject was devised by teachers within the local area of an educational division and so could reflect local methods of teaching and local concerns. As well as testing traditional subjects such as mathematics and English, examinations were also devised for subjects not traditionally associated with examination work, such as metalwork or child care. The first pilot tests took place in June 1952 and June 1953, and in 1953 the South West Hertfordshire Division's Certificate was launched, and began to be accepted by employers; some of the county's other four divisions later awarded their own certificates.

In 1965, the national Certificate of Secondary Education (CSE) was introduced. It was aimed at the same children as the area certificate and based on the methods developed in Hertfordshire and elsewhere. The divisions continued their involvement in examinations by promoting 'mode III' CSE examinations with syllabuses which, like those of the area certificates, were devised by the same teachers who taught them. The 'mode III' examinations also involved much practical and project work, and when CSE and GCE were both replaced by the General Certificate of Secondary Education (first examined in 1988), which also avoided basing the award of a qualification on a single written examination, the experience of those involved in 'mode III' work was drawn upon in turn.

In the early 1960s, discussions were going forward in Hertfordshire on the possible reorganisation of secondary schooling, and in 1964 children in some areas of the county were not allocated to secondary schools on the basis of an examination, but instead were selected after consultation with parents and teachers and after consideration of their primary school record. It was intended that from 1965 no Hertfordshire child should have to sit the 'eleven plus' examination. However, in 1965, all local education authorities were instructed by the government to prepare schemes for the development of all-ability secondary education, and this accelerated Hertfordshire's plans. The county's scheme was approved in 1966 and began to be implemented in 1968 in Welwyn Garden City, followed by Hoddesdon and Broxbourne schools in 1969. The plan aimed to provide five-form entry schools of around 800 to 1,000 pupils, a size which, it was hoped, would be large enough to ensure a good range of courses, but sufficiently small to allow a personal approach and to enable children to feel part of a community. At the time, this proposal for medium-size schools was rather unusual, as it was generally felt that only in larger schools could a complete range of courses be taught. The plan also aimed to allow intake to be determined primarily by parental choice. It was originally aimed to complete the reorganisation by 1973, but even by 1978, only 95 per cent of Hertfordshire secondary schools could cope with a full range of abilities.

In most places, the division of schools under the 1944 Education Act into primary and secondary, with a change of school for every child at the age of eleven, remains an established feature. In 1964, however, local education authorities were given the power to vary this if they wished, and this paved the way for the reorganisation of schools into lower, middle and upper: at the age of nine, children leave their first schools for middle schools, and then move on to upper schools at thirteen. The three-tier system first became operational in Royston in September 1969 and is now operating in the Borehamwood, Berkhamsted, Buntingford and Royston areas. Augustus Smith School, opened in Berkhamsted in 1971, was the first purpose-built middle school in the county.

Hertfordshire has always sought to educate its pupils in practical subjects like sport, craft and rural studies as well as in academic disciplines. One area in which the county has been particularly successful has been in its encouragement of practical music-making. Since 1929 the Rural Music Schools Association at Hitchin (RMSA) had been providing class music teaching and individual instrumental lessons in Hertfordshire schools, as well as evening classes. Then, in 1945, the county established a Music Advisory Committee and the following year H Watkins Shaw began work as the first County Music Organiser. The

School meals at Adeyfield Secondary Modern School, Hemel Hempstead, in 1954.

committee's acknowledged aim was to achieve a piano and a room for music in every school and to develop a gramophone record library and a collection of musical instruments for use by schoolchildren. The RMSA was contracted to continue to provide instrumental lessons, mainly in the north and east of the county, since the Watford School of Music, founded in 1880, was doing similar work in its locality. In 1958 the county took over the work directly and transformed the RMSA's Hitchin school of music into what is now the North Hertfordshire School of Music; the Rural Music Schools Association itself continued its work, however, and has now developed into the residential centre for music courses at Little Benslow Hills, Hitchin. A network of music centres was set up throughout the county, which among other activities ran their own orchestras, while in 1966 the County Youth Orchestra began work under its first conductor Leonard Hirsch.

Further and Higher Education

Before the Second World War, most training colleges for non-graduates were run by the Church of England, like Hockerill College at Bishops Stortford. During and immediately after the war, because of the severe shortage of teachers, a system of 'emergency' training colleges was established to provide 'crash courses', such as that at Little Gaddesden, set up in the former war hospital in the grounds of Ashridge Park. In 1947, the government tried to promote the establishment of permanent training colleges, and established a new national system for funding them. As a result, two colleges were set up in Hertfordshire: Balls Park, in Hertford (opened in 1947) and Wall Hall at Aldenham (opened in 1949, but previously an emergency training college). In addition, in 1953 the County took over the running of the former Froebel Institute college at Offley, which had moved to the county during the war. These colleges produced teachers not just for Hertfordshire schools, but for schools throughout the country. Offley College closed in 1961, but Balls Park and Wall Hall continued their work until 1976, when they were combined into a new College of Higher Education, based at Wall Hall, which aimed to provide a much wider education than a strictly vocational one.

In 1935, the County Council had made plans to build five new technical institutes at Hertford, Barnet, Watford, Welwyn Garden City and Letchworth. Although that at Watford was the only one built before the war, the plan was never completely abandoned, though the most exciting fruit the policy bore was at Hatfield. In 1941 De Havillands of Hatfield, the major aircraft manufacturers (now part of British Aerospace) had set up a technical school for its apprentices, but the training offered was specifically geared to the work of the firm, and it was felt that a wider technical education would be more useful to its students. The chairman of the firm persuaded the County Council that its proposed college in mid-Hertfordshire would be much better situated at Hatfield than at Welwyn Garden City, and he presented the Council with a 90-acre site on which to build it. The college opened in September 1952 with a staff of 30 and 1,500 students, mostly part-time. At first, the college covered work at a range of levels, but by the 1960s it was concentrating on work at the equivalent of degree level. In 1964, the Council for National Academic Awards was created. It had the power to grant degrees, previously the sole province of universities, and led to the creation of the polytechnics, which characteristically provided vocational training leading to the award of a CNAA degree. Hatfield Technical College became one of the first polytechnics, being granted polytechnic status in January 1969. Hertfordshire has no university, though in the 1960s it was hoped that the Chelsea College of Technology would form the nucleus of a university either in Knebworth Park, Stevenage or on a site south of St Albans. Provisional plans were drawn up for both sites, but in the end the college chose to create Brunel University in Uxbridge instead. However, the national reputation which the Hatfield Polytechnic has since made for itself has more than compensated for this lack.

County Library Service

After the war, in common with other County Council services, the County Library experienced a rebirth. A survey of the service made in 1948 identified many problems: there was a lack of central direction and policy, and each branch or library centre was viewed as an isolated unit. The headquarters premises (at County Hall) were inadequate as a central administrative unit, however appropriate they had been for sending out boxes of books. Staff were poorly trained, according to the survey, and more administrative staff were needed.[5] The problems, once identified, began to be solved, and the creation of an integrated library service began.

An important factor in bringing the full resources of the Library Service to all parts of the county has been the development of mobile libraries. The first one, which began operating in November 1949, served not the rural areas generally associated with the use of mobile libraries, but the urban areas of south-west Hertfordshire. It was based at Bushey and served Bushey, Oxhey, Rickmansworth and Carpenders Park. These areas had grown rapidly after the war, particularly the huge London County Council estate at Carpenders Park. There were no buildings in the district suitable for a library, and in any case it was more economic to provide a single mobile library than several part-time branches. It was not until 1954 that the first rural mobile library began to operate in the north Hertfordshire area. It was originally a rather cautious experiment, but its success led to a policy of replacing the 113 village centres with mobile libraries. The process was completed in 1959 with the fifth mobile library beginning work in mid-Hertfordshire, though six rural centres continued to operate, and that at Ashwell still exists. The expansion of the network of branch libraries began in the 1950s too. In 1956 a branch opened in Borehamwood (to serve another London County Council estate) and thereafter the network grew rapidly so that by the 1980s most communities of any size had their own branch.

The service for schools and young people had been practically non-existent before the war, but from the 1940s it too developed rapidly. In 1947 a children's library opened in the Harpenden Library, and in 1948 the first 'Organiser of work with young people' was appointed. Other specialist services emerged, too. Libraries were opened in hospitals and youth clubs as well as in schools. A large music and drama collection was established (held at headquarters until it moved to purpose-built accommodation at Welwyn Garden City in 1974). The County Local Studies collection took longer to develop, but a specialist librarian was finally appointed in 1974. With the growth of further education, and particularly the opening of technical colleges, a specialist technical service was needed. A technical librarian was appointed in 1956 to integrate the technical libraries in colleges throughout the county, and today the service has developed into the HERTIS information service based at Hatfield Polytechnic and serving the county's industrial and commercial interests as much as higher and further education. HERTIS has been recognised as the most effective library cooperation in the United Kingdom, and by 1988 had some 300 companies subscribing to its service, and the largest number of users of any organisation of its type.

In 1965 there was a renewed impetus towards change and development when the 1964 Public Libraries and Museums Act came into force. Under that Act, it became the County Council's duty, not merely its right, to operate a comprehensive library service. The County Library, formerly part of the Education Department, became a department of the County Council in its own right, and the County Librarian a Chief Officer of the County Council. The Library also underwent its own administrative changes, and although it was considered that central co-ordination was still essential, there were now sufficient qualified and experienced staff to enable some responsibilities – such as book purchasing – to be delegated to the three new County Library Divisions for east, mid and west Hertfordshire. By the end of the 1960s, this administrative delegation had become effective, and the headquarters was acting mainly as a bibliographic centre and an administrative centre for book requests and inter-library loans.

Museums

Although under the Public Libraries Act 1919, the County Council had the power to provide museums from the rates, the first three museums in the county – St Albans (opened in 1899), Hertford (1902) and Letchworth (1914) – had been founded and mainly financed by local initiative, and no attempts were made to provide a comprehensive museum service. Even Letchworth Museum's pioneering loan service to schools, begun in 1936, received little support from the County Council until the 1960s. However, new museums were founded through local efforts. The County Council, as the Museum Authority, was by 1960 officially responsible for four of them (Barnet, Hoddesdon, the Rhodes Museum at Bishops Stortford, and Stevenage), though the money it provided was actually paid back by the district councils, who really ran them.

In the 1960s, the County Council began to take a more active role. From 1960 it funded the salary of the first full-time School Service Assistant at Letchworth Museum, to work with schoolchildren visiting the museum and to promote the loans service to schools. It ran the Stevenage and Hoddesdon museums directly from 1965, as it was no longer able (under the provisions of the Libraries and Museums Act 1964) to recharge district councils for museum services. In 1966, the County Librarian presented a report on the provision of museum services identifying the particular problems faced in Hertfordshire, where a comparatively large population was spread between a number of towns, none of which was large enough to act as a museum centre for the whole county, and it proposed that the County Council adopt a co-ordinating role. However, no action was taken by the Library Committee, and it would not be until the 1970s that more positive steps were taken towards the establishment of a comprehensive museums service.

County Architect

Although by 1939 the County Council was responsible for the maintenance of around 300 buildings and had carried out a number of building projects, including smaller schools such as that at Hunsdon (1926), almost all the work had been designed and executed by outside agencies. The County Surveyor acted as County Architect and a small team of architects, surveyors and others worked as a section of the Highways Department. Even County Hall itself, completed in 1939 and the most important project commissioned by the Council so far, was neither designed nor built by Council staff. It was not until 1944 that a full-time County Architect, Charles Aslin, later to be President of the Royal Institute of British Architects, was first appointed, by which time most other counties already had well-developed architects' departments. The establishment of a separate department in Hertfordshire had been proposed in the 1930s, and with the war drawing to a close, it was evident that a huge post-war building programme would be required, particularly for schools, and in order to make sure that building was carried out as quickly and efficiently as possible, it would be essential for the Council to have as close a control as possible over the work.

The raising of the school-leaving age to fifteen in 1947 naturally caused an increase in the school population; the post-war 'baby boom' and the influx of families into Hertfordshire to make their homes in the four new towns and the London County Council housing estates increased it still further. In 1944 the school population was 56,000. By 1954 it had reached 95,000 and was predicted to reach 119,000 by the end of the decade. Furthermore, even before the war, many schools were old and sub-standard; in 1950 it was estimated that half the schools in the county had been built before 1902. An enormous building programme was essential, but with the shortage of materials, the problems of supply and the shortage of skilled labour, at a time when every county was suffering similar problems, it would have been almost impossible to carry out the required programme using conventional building methods. The pioneering solution adopted in Hertfordshire was to develop methods of using pre-fabricated materials – basically steel frames, to which were bolted flat roofs and a variety of concrete wall panels and metal-framed windows and doors. These could be built relatively quickly, using unskilled labour and the materials could be ordered in bulk, not piecemeal for each school. The design of each school, however, was individual, with the architect able to select components from the 'kit of parts'. Unlike existing pre-fabrication schemes which pre-fabricated whole rooms or bays – typified by the 'pre-fab' council houses still evident on some estates today – Hertfordshire standardised smaller components from which rooms of any size were constructed using a standard 'grid' layout. The first post-war primary school, Burleigh School, Cheshunt, was opened in 1948 by R A Butler, Minister of Education 1940–1945; the 100th school built by the new methods in Hertfordshire (Ravenscroft Secondary, New Barnet) was finished in 1954 and by 1961, 200 schools had been completed. At the same time, the design of primary schools underwent an important change: units grouped around a hall cut down on little used corridor space and produced a compact group space for each class, which in the summer could include the outdoor area adjoining each classroom. Architects and teachers worked together on the designs for the schools, ensuring that educational needs were met as closely as possible. An award-winning early example of the method is Templewood School, Welwyn Garden City (1949–1950). Coloured cladding panels and large expanses of glass,

Top; *Templewood School, Welwyn Garden City, an early (1949–50) example of the Hertfordshire County Council's pioneering methods of building construction using pre-fabricated materials.* Bottom; *Hatfield Technical College (now part of Hatfield Polytechnic) soon after it was opened in 1952.*

together with a flat roof (which unfortunately caused initial problems when it leaked) with overhanging eaves characterise the outside of the building. Inside, each classroom is a self-contained unit. There is a corridor, but it is separated from the classrooms only by sliding and folding doors, so that it can become an extension of the teaching space if required, and many of these schools today have exercised the option of converting circulation space for teaching use. Another feature of the Hertfordshire schools was their use of bright colours, inside and out, in complete contrast with the 'institutional' brown and grey paint used in the pre-war schools. Today, the schools and colleges built by this method, with their large expanses of glass and coloured panels, make schools and colleges immediately recognisable, and seem an essential part of the urban (and rural) landscape.

'Hertfordshire' schools were widely publicised and created much interest in architectural circles both nationally and internationally, and their success led to the development of system building methods for schools both in this country and abroad. In 1963, at the request of the Department of Education and Science, Hertfordshire combined with Essex and Kent County Councils and the London Borough of Hillingdon to form the South Eastern Architects' Collaboration (SEAC). Following a precedent of local authority collaboration set in the Midlands and the North of England, the SEAC authorities worked together to purchase and design pre-fabricated components using Hertfordshire's building system and expertise. Pre-fabricated or 'system' building techniques continued to be used in Hertfordshire until the late 1970s – the Hatfield Polytechnic Bio Science and Computer building (1976) was one of the last to be constructed using SEAC components. By this time the amount of new education building required had become too small to make the methods useful, and SEAC was wound up in 1977.

The post-war period, in local government as in so much else, was a time of confidence, expansion and enthusiasm. By the 1970s the mood had become one of uncertainty over jobs, money and about local government itself. Hertfordshire, unlike many other counties, survived the Local Government Act of 1972 unscathed, but even so 1974 marked a new beginning for Hertfordshire and for its Council.

5

Reassessment and a New Beginning 1974–1989

Britain in the 1970s and 1980s has been characterised by inflation and oil crises, unemployment and industrial unrest, public spending cuts and rate-capping. Local authorities and the money they spend came under public scrutiny more than ever before and economising became a way of life. The beginning of the recession was marked by an oil crisis in 1973 and the resulting need to economise on petrol and oil which perhaps set the tone for the years to come. Interest rates rose to unprecedented levels and at the end of the year shops, offices and industrial premises were working a three-day week because of a shortage of electricity caused by industrial action by coal-miners. By 1975 more than 1 million people were unemployed for the first time since the war, and ten years later, over 3 million people were without work. By 1983 the depression seemed to have reached its lowest point. The rate of unemployment (though not the actual numbers of unemployed) began to fall, though since 1981 never fewer than 10 per cent of the working population of Britain have been without work. Much more significant, though, was the distribution of the jobless. It was in the depressed areas of the North and Midlands, where the old industries such as shipbuilding and steel production were declining, that unemployment was concentrated. In Hertfordshire and the rest of the South-east, there was relatively little unemployment; even in Stevenage, with the highest unemployment rate in Hertfordshire, the rate has never approached anywhere near the national figure. Standards of living (and house prices) rose considerably, industry continued to expand and consumer spending was at a high level.

Politically, too, the nation seemed to be becoming polarised. Although support for the Labour Party has traditionally been working class, it has been represented in all areas of Britain. In the general election in May 1979 which brought the Conservative Party and Margaret Thatcher to power, the swing of 4 per cent of support towards the Conservative Party was very much higher in the South-east; in Hertfordshire the two sitting Labour MPs were defeated, including the popular Shirley Williams (Stevenage) and since then the county has been represented at Westminster only by Conservatives. In the 1981 local government elections, which demonstrated a swing of support towards the Labour Party, the swing was stronger in the North; and in the 1987 general election the North/South divide was even more pronounced, with Labour holding only 26 of the 260 seats south of a line from the Severn to the Wash.

Local Government Reorganisation

It was in this context of inflation and depression that local government in England and Wales underwent radical changes. Since the 1940s, a reorganisation of local government on a 'single-tier' system had been discussed. Since the Second World War, the district councils (which formed the third tier, beneath the top tier represented by central government and the second tier of the county councils) had increasingly had their jurisdiction weakened by the transfer to the county councils of such functions as fire services, police and education. The small district councils in particular were felt to be inefficient and the division of functions unwieldy and unintelligible. In 1965 a Local Government Commission was appointed under the chairmanship of Lord Redcliffe-Maud, and in its report published in 1966 it proposed a radical restructuring of local government in England and Wales. Fifty-eight 'unitary authorities' were proposed, each larger than the current district councils but smaller than most counties. Under the scheme, Hertfordshire would have been divided between two authorities: East Hertfordshire (including west Essex) and West Hertfordshire (including Luton), though Royston and the surrounding areas would have been transferred to area 42 (Cambridge and the south Fens) and the Tring area to mid-Buckinghamshire. Given the disruption which local government reorganisation was in any case to cause, and the problems which have continued to arise in many areas as a result of the two-tier system, it is perhaps unfortunate that the scheme was not implemented. However, the Labour Government which intended to introduce the scheme was defeated at the 1970 general election and – though local government reform was not mentioned in the election campaign – the new Conservative Government introduced a completely different, two tier, scheme.

Under the Local Government Act of 1972, the old boroughs and urban and rural districts were swept away and replaced with new, larger, districts. In Hertfordshire, four boroughs, nineteen urban and twelve rural districts were replaced by just ten new local authorities. In the big cities like Manchester and Birmingham, new metropolitan counties were formed, together with new 'shire' counties, like Avon. Old counties like Huntingdonshire and Rutland, which had existed as administrative units since before the time of Domesday Book, disappeared, to great public outcry. The administrative areas of almost all the other counties in England and Wales were altered; only Hertfordshire and four other counties – Cornwall, the Isle of Wight, Salop (Shropshire) and Wiltshire – retained their old boundaries. Other changes took place at the same time. The Local Government Commission for Administration – more popularly known as the Local Government Ombudsman – was created. The National Health Service was restructured. New Area Health Authorities co-terminous with the new counties were created and some functions formerly carried out by county councils, such as the child and school health service and the ambulance service were removed from local to central government.

The New Hertfordshire County Council

Even where a county itself did, like Hertfordshire, remain intact, the effect of the Act was still to terminate the existence of the old County Council and replace it with a new one, which took power on 1 April 1974. In Hertfordshire, this coincided with a change in the legal name of the County Council. The old Council had officially been 'the County Council for the County of Hertford', whereas now there was actually a 'Hertfordshire County Council' – the name by which the old Council had been generally known for many years. The new Council began work a full year before the old Council 'died' on 31 March 1974. Elections for the new Hertfordshire County Council took place on 12 April 1973 and the Council met for the first time on 17 April.

Nationally, there was a general swing to Labour, which won the GLC from the Conservatives and was particularly successful in the new metropolitan counties. In Hertfordshire, even the leader of the Conservative/Independent group of the old County Council was defeated. Although many of the 'new' County Councillors were also members of the old Council, its composition was very different. Of the 72 seats on the new Council, the Labour Party and the Conservatives each took 33, with one independent, one ratepayers association member and four Liberals. For the first time ever, Hertfordshire had a hung Council in which the Conservatives did not have a clear majority. It was not obvious where the balance of power would lie – nor even from which party the Chairman of the Council would be chosen – and the County Secretary even had under his desk a bag and two billiard balls in case of deadlock! The question was resolved at the second Council meeting on 24 May, when County Councillor Philip Ireton was elected the first Labour Chairman of a Hertfordshire County Council, beating the Chairman of the 'old' Council by just 37 votes to 35. Because the Liberals would not ally themselves permanently with either of the two major parties, the chairmanships of the various committees were split between members of the Conservative and Labour groups.

Although administratively the changeover from the old to the new County Council was remarkably smooth, the next few years were not easy for the senior staff of the County Council. Quite apart from carrying out the changes in administrative structure and working practices resulting from reorganisation itself and the attendant changes in the County Council's powers and duties, officers were for a year working for two County Councils simultaneously, each of a different political composition. Even after the old Council ceased to exist, they still had the difficult task of working for a hung Council, where a decision made by a sub-committee dominated by one party might be overturned by a committee on which the other party had the balance of power, or by the full Council. For the elected members, the experience of a hung Council had focussed attentions sharply on their political affiliations. Since that time, the party group structure has continued to develop so that now policy developed by the national party organisation has (at least for Conservative and Labour members) become a much more significant factor in the decision-making process than it had ever been in the old County Council.

The new county councils are subject to re-election every four years. In the 1977 elections in Hertfordshire the Conservatives more than made up the ground they had lost in 1973, and the Labour membership was drastically reduced to only six. The following election, in 1981, saw the Conservatives lose ground slightly, but they retained a comfortable majority. Following the 1985 elections, however, Hertfordshire once again had a 'hung' County Council: 36 Conservatives, 27 Labour and 14 members of the Liberal/SDP Alliance (now the Democrats), who now began to be accepted as an independent third party. A combination of any two parties could defeat the third. For two years the Conservatives retained their chairmanships of the Council and its committees, but in 1987 the chairs of all committees passed to the Labour group. It is a significant indication of how important the party structure had become, that this time there was no question of sharing power between the two main parties.

For the elected councillors, the character of the Council changed considerably after 1974. There were no longer aldermen, who had been chosen by the councillors themselves in recognition of their service to the county. Although this did mean the loss of some respected figures, the aldermanic system had enabled some people to remain on the Council after they had reached an age when they might better have retired, and the loss of the aldermen immediately lowered the average age of the Council. More younger councillors are now being elected, and more women. The Council is becoming more representative of the community it serves, though many feel that it is still too male-dominated and too old. Councillors still tend to be the self-employed, the retired or those working at home and it seems to be difficult to encourage different types of people to stand for election. Those who are elected have far more to do than simply attend Council and committee meetings. Partly because of the 'balanced' Council, and partly because the Council now takes itself much more seriously as a professional decision-making body, issues are examined in much greater depth. Before each committee meeting there are important 'briefing meetings' for each party to discuss the major issues with the Chief Officers involved. By the time of the committee meeting Councillors are already fully informed on the matters to be discussed and groups have already decided their own policy. On some matters (such as, for example, a minor road improvement such as a mini-roundabout or a pedestrian crossing) members and officers will have discussed the matter with local residents and relevant officers before the matter is taken to committee, while on major issues such as school closures, members as well as officers are involved in seeking local opinions. Despite all this work out of the formal Council and committee meetings, County Council meetings have become longer and longer, simply because there is now so much business to transact. Before 1974, meetings of the full Council often lasted only a few hours. Now, meetings which begin at 10.00am normally extend well into the evening, and on occasions might have been better carried into a second day.

Internal Organisation

The new County Council inherited most of the staff and much of the organisation of the old. Suggestions for the administrative structure of the new local authorities had been made in the Bains Report. For the completely new authorities, it was relatively straightforward to adopt the Bains suggestions, but in Hertfordshire, where it would have been possible to carry on the administration very much as before, there was much debate on the question.

Bains proposed the formation of directorates, with services divided into large groups. In Hertfordshire, five large groupings were considered for a time: education; social services (both as before); land use, transportation and the environment; community facilities (such as libraries) and operational services (police, fire, trading standards). In the end, however, the division of the Council's work into departments remained basically the same as before. Eleven Chief Officers were appointed, each with their own department (plus the Chief Constable, who is not appointed directly by the County Council). All Chief Officers had to re-apply for their posts, but some chose to retire. For the new post of Chief Executive, the former Clerk of the County Council, Peter Boyce, found himself competing (successfully) against about 200 other applicants.

The Health Department was the only one to disappear altogether at the time of reorganisation. Since 1897 the county had had a Medical Officer of Health, but now all the county's remaining medical and nursing functions passed to the Area Health Authorities. Only a handful of public health responsibilities remained, and these were given to a newly created Environmental Health Section (later the Environmental Services Unit) of the County Secretary's Department. Since 1974, the County Council's departmental structure has worked reasonably efficiently, despite enormous variations in size, with its smallest department, the County Record Office, having just fourteen staff and an annual budget of under £200,000 and the largest, Education, employing 12,500 teaching staff and 16,500 others and spending nearly £300m a year. There has only been one major change in the structure, when in 1986 the Planning and Land Agent's departments merged to form a new Planning and Estates Department. Another is planned for 1989, when a new Information Systems Directorate (incorporating the computer division of the Finance Department and the Management Services Unit of the County Secretary's Department) will begin work.

One of the central proposals of the Bains Report was that councils should pay more attention to the concept of corporate management for the whole authority. In order to achieve this, it would be necessary to appoint an officer with oversight of the administration as a whole. In the past, in Hertfordshire as elsewhere, the Clerk had usually played a co-ordinating role. This tended to place the Clerk's Department, with its own particular functions, on a different footing from the other departments, which was not always satisfactory. Eventually it was decided to appoint a Chief Executive who would oversee the whole administration without having a department of his own to run as well. The Clerk of the County Council became the County Secretary, with a department on the same level as all the others. Because of its general legal and administrative role, the County Secretary's department has, however, continued to dominate, and so in recent years there has been in many authorities a tendency for the Chief Executive to become once more identified with the secretariat. This has not happened in Hertfordshire, but as elsewhere a central press office and policy unit have evolved to strengthen the corporate management. The Chief Executive, who initially had no department of his own, now has a small Policy Co-ordination Unit reporting directly to him and will, from 1989, similarly have an Information Technology Strategy Unit.

Although the departmental structure of the administration remained basically unchanged, the County Council's committee structure was completely revised. In place of the fifteen committees of the old County Council, ten committees were established: three to deal with matters affecting the County Council generally, including its finances, staff and internal administration, and the remainder to cover its services, which were divided into seven areas. Under the old County Council, each committee had generally represented the work of one department, but in the new system, the correspondence was less close. The largest departments (Education, Social Services, Highways and the Police) did continue to have a corresponding committee, but the other three committees covered the work of all the remaining departments. The Fire and Public Protection Committee, for example, dealt with consumer protection, emergency planning, and licensing as well as exercising the Council's duties as fire authority.

Government Control

A major feature of local, and particularly county, government since 1974 has been the high degree of central government control and direction, especially in financial matters. This has, perhaps, been even more significant in the more wealthy counties like Hertfordshire, where the proportion of County Council expenditure funded by the government's block grant has declined every year from 1975/76. The distribution of grant depends on the government's assessment of an authority's 'need to spend', based on population and other factors, and on the level of rateable values as a measure of the ratepayers' ability to pay. Since Hertfordshire has a low assessed 'needs' level and since rateable values are relatively high, the county has continually lost grant. In the financial year 1975/76, 52 per cent of county expenditure was funded by block grant; in 1988/89 Hertfordshire received no block grant at all. Even if the County Council spent at the level which the government believes it should in the year 1988/89, it would only have received £28.1 million in grant (6.3 per cent of net expenditure), and for the year 1989/90 the county would receive no grant even if it did keep its spending down to the government's assessed level. Though the proportion of total local authority expenditure financed by the block grant has declined, 46.4 per cent of expenditure as a whole in 1987/88 was still funded by block grant.

However, central government has been spending less and less on local government generally. The overall level of government expenditure as a proportion of Gross Domestic Product (GDP) fell from 1982/83 and it is intended to reduce this proportion still further. In parallel with this national trend, central government has made continuous attempts to reduce the amount local authorities spend. Various measures have been used: a new grant system in 1981/82 which included a penalty system for high spending authorities; limits on capital spending; the Ratecapping Act of 1984, under which the government could fix maximum permitted levels of rates (though Hertfordshire was not affected). Moves were made towards more specific grants for particular services and local authorities were required to produce annual reports to inform ratepayers on how money was spent. In 1982 the Audit Commission was created, to monitor and investigate local authority expenditure and advise how resources could be used more effectively. Although overall the effect of these controls has not significantly reduced local authority spending as a proportion of GDP, different local authorities are affected to different extents, and Hertfordshire has suffered more than most.

Education

Education has continued to be the aspect of the County Council's work which affects the most people and which has taken the largest proportion of the Council's resources. It was little affected by the reorganisation of local government, though the Education Committee had even more power of decision-making once the remaining five Divisional Executives to which it had delegated various functions were wound up, retaining the local offices for administrative purposes only.

The biggest factor affecting education in the period has been demographic change. As the 'bulge' generation passed through the schools a huge expansion in the provision of educational facilities was necessary; as it has grown older the numbers on roll have fallen. Nearly 15,500 children entered secondary schools in 1974, but by 1986 the number had fallen to 10,700. Between 1976 and 1988, 25 Hertfordshire schools have had to be closed, both secondary and primary, amid much controversy concerning which should be the unfortunate schools destined for closure. In Stevenage, to take just one example, the effects have been particularly noticeable because in its early years as a new town it attracted a high proportion of young families, and to accommodate the large school-age population a considerable number of schools were built. As rolls fell, Shephalbury and Chells secondary schools closed first, with the Nobel School moving to the Chells site. The Shephalbury site continued in use for education purposes as part of the Stevenage College, but the Nobel site was sold to the borough council for community use. Next came the amalgamation of the girls' and boys' Roman Catholic schools, with the site of the former boys' school being destined for use for housing; and the amalgamation of the long-established Alleynes School for boys and the much newer Stevenage Girls School is due to take place in 1989. Many other communities have been similarly, though less drastically, affected by school closures. Although individual communities may seem to suffer from school closures, education provision as a whole has benefited from the opportunity to match the number of places available to the number of pupils, and school buildings no longer required have become available for alternative educational use, such as for teachers' centres.

Particularly since the 1970s, views about the education of children and young people with special learning needs have changed fundamentally. The 1981 Education Act stipulates that as far as possible the needs of these students should be met within ordinary schools and colleges. In 1986 a review of provision for children and young people with special educational needs was carried out in Hertfordshire. As far as is practical their needs are met within mainstream schools and colleges in the county. The needs of some children with moderate or severe learning difficulties are best met in special schools. These schools aim to provide a balanced curriculum but also to establish purposeful links with ordinary schools and colleges.

Educational methods and concerns have never remained static, and perhaps the most exciting development of the last few years, and one in which Hertfordshire has been a national pioneer, has been the Technical and Vocational Education Initiative (TVEI). The aim of the initiative is to provide a curriculum covering a range of vocationally relevant skills including manufacturing technology, information technology and computer studies. Work experience is an important element, and the consequent involvement of commerce and industry has been typical of the period not just in connection with education but also in other aspects of the County Council's work. Despite the support of industry, it has not been possible to provide all pupils with work experience placements in commercial organisations, so fourth- and fifth-year pupils in Stevenage also undertake simulated work experience in the County Council's own Hertfordshire Youth Technology and Enterprise Centre (HYTEC). The centre acts as a manufacturing company, creating products and providing services, and pupils working there develop their skills in such areas as graphic design, desktop publishing and catering as well as becoming involved in management decisions and problem-solving. The original TVEI project, which was funded by government money, began in 1983 when Hertfordshire was chosen as one of just fourteen education authorities to benefit from the five-year pilot scheme. It was decided that most benefit would be derived by concentrating the experiment in one area, so each of the ten secondary schools in Stevenage participated. The project expanded to Letchworth, Baldock and Royston in 1983 and now covers the whole county; Hertfordshire is one of only a few education authorities to have implemented TVEI so fully.

Higher Education, too, has undergone many changes. In particular, the Hatfield Polytechnic has expanded considerably. In 1976, the two former Colleges of Education, Balls Park in Hertford and Wall Hall at Aldenham were combined to form the Hertfordshire College of Higher Education, the aim of which was to provide not only vocational training for teachers but an all-round higher education as well. The choice of site was much disputed, and there was intense campaigning by the students and staff of both Wall Hall and Balls Park Colleges, each of whom wanted their site to become the home of the new college. The Education Committee eventually decided by just one vote to use the Wall Hall site. The Balls Park site was transferred to the ever-expanding polytechnic, becoming its School of Business and Social Sciences. The Hertfordshire College did not survive for long, for in April 1987 it too was absorbed into the polytechnic. There has been development, too, at the polytechnic's original site at Hatfield, including the Bio Science and Computer block opened in 1976 and the Students' Communal Building. In 1989 the polytechnic, for nearly 40 years a symbol of the best in Hertfordshire's educational provision, becomes, with its fellow polytechnics, an independent institution.

As well as the polytechnic, the County Council now has twelve further education colleges, including the specialist colleges of agriculture, art, and building. As well as catering for those who continue their studies immediately after school, the colleges provide important opportunities for adults who wish to continue their education either full- or part-time.

The further development of the county's education service will take place in the context of the most profound legislative change since the 1944 Education Act. Under the 1988 Education Act, a national curriculum will be introduced, with nationally determined attainment targets and assessments at the ages of 7, 11, 14 and 16. There will also be much more delegation to individual schools in financial and staffing matters. At the same time, the 1988 Local Government Act will, amongst other provisions, introduce compulsory competition for the provision of school meals, cleaning and grounds maintenance, all of which are currently carried out by Education Department staff.

Social Services

The Social Services had undergone reorganisation in 1971 when the department was created by the merger of the Children's Department and the Health and Welfare Department, so there was little change in 1974. The department was responsible for providing care and support for a wide range of people: children at risk and their families; children and young people in trouble with the law; the elderly; people with a mental handicap, the physically disabled and the mentally ill, together with those suffering from drug or alcohol abuse, and gypsies. The aim of the department was to benefit all these disparate classes by means of an integrated social service, which consulted its clients, as those who benefited from the service increasingly became known. Since 1974, social services departments have become increasingly prominent nationally, with considerable publicity being given to their activities. There have been 23 public inquiries in Britain since 1974 relating to the activities of social services departments, the latest – possibly the longest and most expensive public inquiry ever held in this country – being the Cleveland child abuse inquiry.

The elderly were a particular concern of the department from the 1970s: in 1974 a special research project on old age in Hertfordshire was carried out by the

The Social Services Department's Home Care Service enables elderly people to remain independent in their own homes.

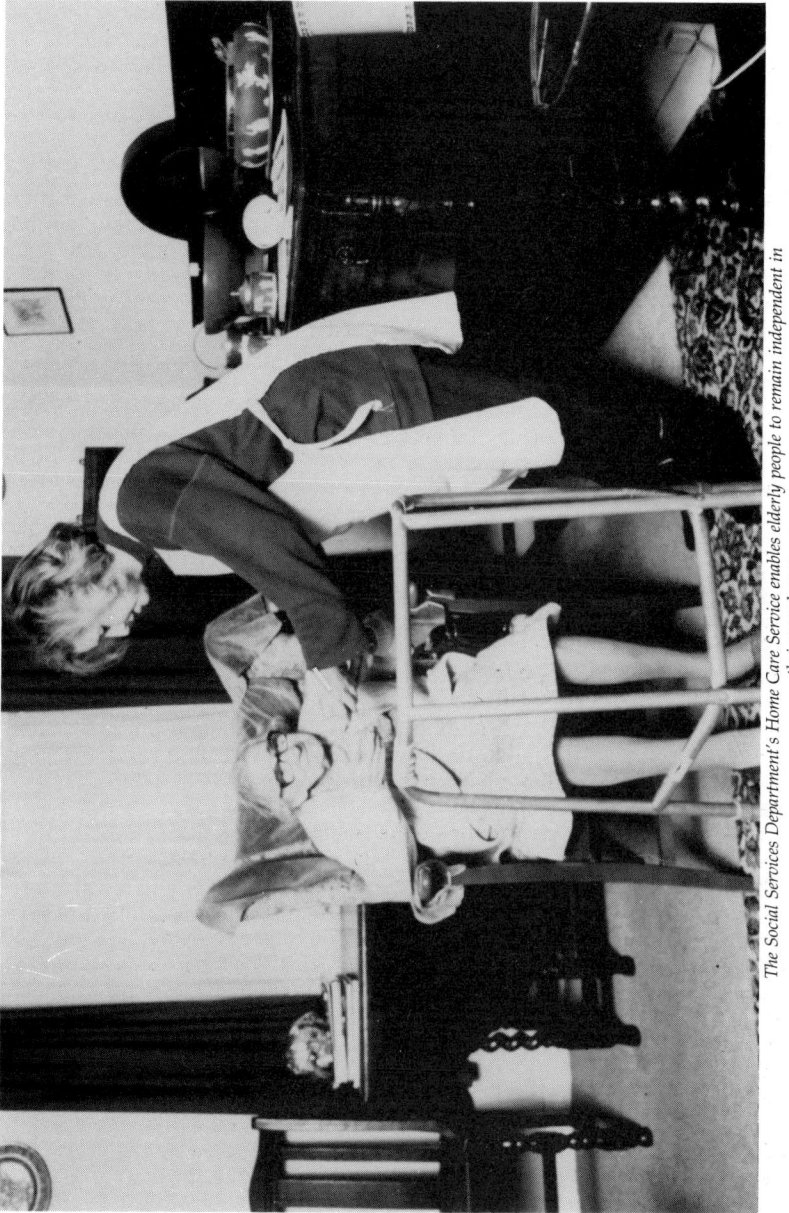

Social Services Committee in collaboration with Hatfield Polytechnic and Cassio College, Watford, which revealed that most elderly people would prefer, not surprisingly, to be cared for in their own homes, rather than being removed to hospital or to a residential institution when they were unable to care for themselves. By the 1980s, even more emphasis was placed on the elderly, and particular thought has been given to the care of the very elderly – those over 85, who are the most likely to need special care. In 1971, about 0.7 per cent of the population were over 85; the proportion has grown steadily so that by the late 1980s, about 1 in every 100 people is over 85 years old; it is predicted that between 1988 and 1998 the number of over-85s will rise to 1.7 per cent. In order to enable people to stay in their own homes as far as possible, the department has developed a Home Care Service provided by specially trained domiciliary assistants who provide a level of care suited to individual needs, including visiting night and morning to help people get up and go to bed.

At the other extreme of age, the department cares for children and their families in a range of circumstances. Already by 1974 the department had long practised the policy of helping families in difficulty to stay together wherever possible, rather than removing children into care. Even when removal from the parents is regarded as being in the best interests of a child, the aim is still to place the child with a foster family rather than in institutional care. However, there are still many children who are hard to place with foster parents – the mentally or physically handicapped, or teenagers who are too old for conventional fostering. It was with the needs of such children particularly in mind that the Social Services Department's Family Finders 'shop' was opened in 1985. Although carrying on much of the conventional adoption and fostering work which the department had done for many years, the 'shop' has deliberately dissociated its image from the County Council's official face. Its premises in Hertford's town centre provide a friendlier atmosphere than was possible at County Hall, and it uses advertisements in its shop window both to find families for individual children and to promote the welfare of children generally.

An important aspect of the department's work has been the increasing care of people within the community, which is in extreme contrast with the earlier policy of placing people in large, often isolated, institutions together with others with similar needs. This applies not only to the elderly and children but, for example, to those with physical disabilities for whom day centres are provided with specialist equipment. An experimental 'dial-a-ride' scheme began in one area of the county in 1987 for people unable to use public transport or ordinary cars: soon after the service began more than 200 people had registered for the service which was running 40 journeys a week in two purpose-built vehicles with tail-lifts.

The mentally handicapped have benefited from this thinking too, and the Social Services Department has worked with the Regional Health Authority to help people move from large hospitals such as Cell Barnes or Leavesden into small homes within the community. Many mentally handicapped people live with their parents and help and support is given to the carers as well as to the handicapped people themselves. One aspect of this has been the 'respite care' scheme which enables carers to go on holiday while their charges are looked after.

Although the county lost most of its remaining health functions as a result of local government reorganisation, the Social Services began to work even more closely with the National Health Service in several areas. Before 1974, hospital social workers had been employed by the National Health Service, but from that date these social workers – 38 staff in Hertfordshire – were transferred to the Social Services Department, becoming part of the integrated social-work team. In 1974 too, a joint consultative committee was set up with the Area Health Authority (since replaced by District Health Authorities) to co-ordinate work, while the child abuse teams set up in 1975 (as a result of the report into the death of Maria Colwell while in the care of the East Sussex County Council), worked to an Area Committee which included nurses, general practicioners and psychiatrists as well as representatives of the police and the NSPCC. In 1986, the Social Services Department underwent a major reorganisation in which more local offices were established within a structure of four areas, each corresponding to a Health Authority area.

The problems of gypsies are rather different from those of most Social Services Department clients, and both before and after 1974 much thought, discussion and controversy has been spent on the question of how best to provide for gypsies and their families. The 1968 Caravan Sites Act required county councils to provide adequate accommodation for gypsies 'residing in or resorting to their area'. Hertfordshire had established its first site, one of the first in the country, at Holwell (between Hatfield and Hertford) as long ago as 1964, and by 1974 there were already sites in several areas of the county. After 1974, much thought and discussion went into the problem of how best to provide for gypsies and their families, including how best to educate their children. By 1988, there were nine County Council sites, situated in six of the ten districts, providing 148 pitches (each for one family, who may have more than one caravan). In general, Hertfordshire has preferred to encourage gypsy children to attend the ordinary schools, though there have been some experiments with mobile schools.

Police

After 1974, the police force continued as a county service, under a Police Committee composed of members of the County Council and of Hertfordshire magistrates; though as with all police forces it is also subject to some control by the Home Office.

As elsewhere in England, the crime rate in Hertfordshire has risen to worrying proportions, and there has been particular concern at the increase in crimes of violence. Between 1984 and 1986, to take just one example, the number of cases of robbery where shotguns or hand guns were used rose from 25 to 45 cases – an alarming 181 per cent. Crime is not the only concern of the police force. With over 2,000 miles of roads in the county, 143 of them motorways (counting each carriageway separately), traffic patrolling is another increasingly significant aspect of the force's work. In 1986 both the A1(M) Hatfield Tunnel and the final section of the M25 motorway opened, resulting in greatly increased traffic flows through the county: soon after its opening, traffic flows on the M25 were already exceeding, by 10,000 vehicles a day, the estimated flow for the year 2001. With more and faster cars in the county there has been an increase in serious accidents. In 1986, for example, there were 69 fatal accidents in Hertfordshire resulting in the deaths of 76 people, and a major cause of accidents has been drunken driving.

One weapon used by the police to deal more effectively with both the growing crime rate and the increasing traffic problems has been the introduction of new technology. In 1986, a new command and operations wing (designed by the County Architect's Department) was opened at Police Headquarters in Welwyn Garden City. Amongst its many facilities for monitoring and controlling communications throughout the county is closed circuit television monitoring of traffic in the Hatfield Tunnel, and in the event of an emergency the amount of lighting and ventilation in the tunnel can be increased directly from the control room. In 1987 a new centralised computer system came into operation, including a link to the police national computer, which by January 1988 was in use by police divisions throughout the county. In the same year the Hertfordshire Police began to use a computer system for the management of serious crime investigations – the Home Office Large Major Enquiry System (HOLMES!).

However sophisticated the equipment used, it is not on its own able to tackle crime at its root. Accordingly, policing is now being taken back into the community. The 'unit policing' of the 1960s, using the rather anonymous police cars, has been phased out, and police inspectors have begun to be identified with particular areas instead of particular shifts. Another attempt to improve community relations was made in 1983 when nine consultative committees were set up throughout the county to act as a forum for comment about policing in their areas. As the alarming increase in crime has continued, and it has been recognised that its reduction depends on more than increased manning levels, the police are promoting self-help schemes like Neighbourhood Watch. By 1987 there were 1,206 such schemes operating in Hertfordshire, emphasising the current view that however efficient and sophisticated the police force, the responsibility for fighting crime rests ultimately with each individual.

Fire Brigade

In 1974, the Ambulance Service passed to the Area Health Authority, although some fire stations continued to be shared as ambulance stations. At the same time the former fire and ambulance workshop at Hatfield was combined with the Highways Department workshop to become a single corporate resource available to all county vehicles. The Fire Service continued to develop, and one of the ways it increased its efficiency was through improved communications. In 1973, a fourth floor was added to the Fire Brigade Headquarters building to house the new computerised central control room. The system was updated in 1985 and now uses the most advanced technology to monitor and control the position of all appliances and personnel and ensure the quickest and most efficient response to any call.

Although the number of firemen has increased since the early days of the Fire Brigade, the proportion of part-time retained firemen has fallen considerably. In the year 1949/50, there were 189 full-time men and 437 part-time retained men who were called out from their place of work as they were needed. By 1978, there were only 188 retained men to 444 full-time, though in recent years the numbers of both full and part-time firemen have risen (237 retained; 558 full-time in 1988). The retained personnel have remained an essential element of the service, providing immediate response to emergencies in smaller and more rural communities, and providing back-up to whole-time crews in urban areas. Recruitment to the retained force has, however, become harder to achieve as the nature of daily work has changed and as people increasingly work at a distance from their homes.

The number of incidents dealt with by the brigade has increased much more than the strength of personnel. In the first year of the brigade's existence, 2,193 calls were received, and the number has risen steadily, with over 6,000 calls in 1968 and nearly 10,000 in 1987/88. The actual number of turnouts in 1987/88, including calls from neighbouring counties, was nearly 17,000 – many calls result in more than one appliance turning out. The Fire Brigade has been increasingly developing the expertise to answer 'special service calls', rescuing people (or animals) from the wreckage of a road accident, or dealing with accidents involving flood or collapsed buildings or earthworks. Even the proverbial cat is still sometimes rescued from a tree! Chemical incidents, unheard of in 1948, are becoming increasingly common and increasingly hazardous and require ever more sophisticated equipment and protective clothing to tackle them effectively.

Despite the vast increase in the number of fires reported, it is interesting to see the reduction in the numbers of chimney fires with the advent of domestic central heating. In the first decade of the Brigade's life, these rose from 590 a year in 1948/49 to 1,172 a year in 1958/59, but in 1969 had declined to 808, and in the year 1987/88 fewer than 300 chimney fires were reported. Sadly, the number of false alarms of malicious origin (as opposed to genuine mistakes) increased even more rapidly than the number of genuine calls, from 99 in 1948/49 to over 540 in 1968/69 and over 800 malicious calls in 1987/88.

Fire protection has increased to become an important aspect of the Brigade's work. During the year 1987/88, nearly 700 full surveys of shops, factories and other premises were made, and nearly 6,000 other visits, so that now around 19,000 premises have been inspected by the Fire Service at some time. With the recent Fire Safety and Safety at Places of Sport Act, this work will increase dramatically over the next few years. The promotion of fire safety generally is also important. In 1987 Welephant, the large red elephant whose aim in life is to make children (and adults) aware of the dangers of fire, made his first visit to Hertfordshire, and as well as its own Welephant suit, the brigade now has a new mobile exhibition unit, which includes television and video equipment.

The work of the Fire Brigade, like that of the Police and Ambulance services, is frequently taken for granted by the people whom it protects, but in 1977 when many Hertfordshire firemen joined the national strike in pursuit of the Fire Brigade Union's claim for a £20 a week pay rise, at a time when a fully trained leading fireman might earn £68 for a 48-hour week, many were forced to realise how much they depended on having a skilled fire-fighting force on call 24 hours a day. The strike lasted from 14 November 1977 until 16 January 1978, with all twelve of the whole-time stations and one of the four day-manning stations out of use. During this period twelve 'Green Goddess' fire engines manned by servicemen supported the retained stations, which continued to work normally.

Some of the incidents attended by the Fire Brigade during the last 40 years have had their humorous aspects, but many have involved tragedy and loss of life to members of the public and even to the fire-fighters. About five firemen in Britain die every year while in the course of their duties. In October 1987, for example, a Hertfordshire fireman, Stuart Lough, died when his emergency rescue tender hit a tree on the way to answer a call to a road accident. This places great stress on Fire Brigade personnel, and in recent years efforts have been made nationally to evaluate and alleviate its effect. In 1983, the Hertfordshire Fire Brigade appointed its first chaplain, a uniformed fire officer, to address the pastoral needs of the Fire Brigade; he is one of only two chaplains who serve as uniformed members of a Fire Service.

During its 40 years of life, the Hertfordshire Fire Brigade has seen a continual increase in the number of incidents, in their scale and in the pressures and danger they place on the fire-fighters, but the Brigade's essential role – to protect the public with a professional and efficient fire-fighting force – remains unchanged.

Highways

The major concern for the Highways Department after 1974 continued to be the growth of traffic in the county, and the consequent building of more roads. Congestion in towns was relieved by the building of more bypasses, such as those for Stanstead Abbots, Bishops Stortford, Ware, Puckeridge and the recent one at Buntingford. The aim has been to establish a network of main roads sufficient to cover the county and discourage the use of minor roads, but as the main roads themselves become congested, motorists take once again to these minor roads and the unresolved dilemma is then whether to improve these minor roads, thus encouraging more traffic, or to leave them to deteriorate still further with the increasing volume of traffic they have to carry. One partial solution which Hertfordshire had to take earlier than many counties because of the sheer quantity of traffic, was to ban lorries and other heavy vehicles from certain roads, and encourage them to take specially designated lorry routes.

As well as building county roads, the Highways Department has been involved in the construction of major trunk roads. Initially such work was done by the Road Construction Unit attached to the department, whose staff worked exclusively for the Department of Transport, and after 1980 when the units were wound up, by the department itself as agent for the Department of Transport. The widening of the M1 motorway was one such major project, and even more important was the building of the A1(M) Hatfield Tunnel. The 1,100 metre tunnel, the longest cut-and-cover road tunnel in Europe, which cost £70m to build, opened in December 1986. It represented the final section of the A1(M) motorway in Hertfordshire and with the commercial and industrial development which will eventually be built on top of it has been hailed as a model of integrated urban development.

It is not enough to construct new roads; the existing network must be maintained along with its street lighting, signs and signals. The considerable growth in economic activity in Hertfordshire since 1974 has resulted in increasing traffic volumes, particularly in heavy commercial vehicles, which has caused continuous wear on the county's highways and an increase in the cost of maintenance from £7m in 1982 to over £40m in 1988. The Highways Department has (like other County Council services) met this challenge partly by using new technology, which improves its ability to assess maintenance needs and work priorities. The HERMIS management information system holds inventory data on all county roads and allows a systematic approach to assessment of new schemes and allocation of budgets. Mini weather stations linked to a central computer and to the London Weather Centre assist in deciding when to salt the roads during winter.

With more and faster traffic, roads have become ever more dangerous, and road safety work has received high priority. In 1974 a road safety engineering team was formed to develop techniques for accident investigation and the treatment of accident blacksites. By 1980 the county had achieved a high reputation both nationally and internationally in this work. Details of individual accidents and patterns of accidents are studied to establish common elements which could relate to the road layout. In this way significant reductions in the number of accidents have been achieved by relatively low cost engineering measures. These can include things like hatch markings to help motorists turning right or painting white lines to mark the edges of roads. Experiments began in the early 1970s with mini-roundabouts, which have proved effective and economic solutions to many junction problems.

The work of road safety education, publicity and training was carried out from 1968 as part of the work of the Emergency Planning Department, but in 1984 the team moved to the Highways Department. It is essential that road safety training education starts at the youngest possible age and there is a programme of work starting with pre-school groups and going right through to the time that pupils leave school. All aspects of road safety are covered, from crossing the road and cycling proficiency training (over 100,000 children were trained

The A1(M) tunnel under construction at Hatfield. The 1100m tunnel was opened in December 1986.

between 1974 and 1988) to pre-driver training and the dangers of drinking and driving. Traditionally this work has taken place outside the curriculum, but the Hertfordshire approach seeks to integrate road safety into the curriculum of both primary and secondary schools. Adults of course benefit too, and advanced driver and advanced motor cycle courses attract over 300 people a year. More recently, seminars have begun to be held for groups such as transport managers, with the aim of promoting advanced driving training for professional drivers. The success of the department's work in this field is borne out by the statistics: in the twenty years from 1965 (when figures began to be computerised) to 1985, the amount of traffic in Hertfordshire has doubled, but the number of accidents has been reduced by 20 per cent.

Since 1974, the Highways Department has been responsible for disposing of the waste collected by district councils – previously each district had made its own arrangements. The amount of rubbish increases every year faster than the population grows, and basically it is disposed of by filling large holes in the ground. Despite the amount of gravel extraction in Hertfordshire, sites suitable for waste disposal are at a premium and are generally owned and run as commercial concerns. Many of the commercially run sites in Hertfordshire receive rubbish from London, which makes it even harder to find space for Hertfordshire's own waste, which currently amounts to around 375,000 tons a year – about a third of a ton per head of population. The County Council inherited only one site in 1974, at Much Hadham, and in 1979 it was decided that although in the east of the county this site and commercial sites could be used, in the west rubbish would have to be shipped elsewhere. A temporary transfer station was established near Radlett, which in 1983 was replaced by a purpose-built one at Waterdale, near Watford, where rubbish is packed into lorries and sent into sites in Bedfordshire. Although relatively expensive to run, this has proved an effective way of disposing of the waste from western Hertfordshire. The department also runs (either directly or via agents) nineteen household waste sites where householders can take bulky waste and garden rubbish for disposal.

Planning

The County Council's planning functions underwent considerable changes as a result of local government reorganisation. The new district councils became responsible both for development control and for compiling local land use plans, functions which were previously exercised by the County Council. The County Council was still responsible for the preparation of a Structure Plan (a strategic plan for the whole county), and was also to deal with planning applications concerning mineral workings or those which concerned uses of land inconsistent with the County Structure Plan or a district plan. The districts also took responsibility for conservation areas and listed building control, though the County Council has continued to offer help to the districts and to the public through its specialist conservation team.

Since 1974, the work of the Planning Department developed in a wide variety of new areas. The County Council had for many years concerned itself with the county's environment generally, but now it was able to take much more initiative in its management. In 1976, for example, the Hertfordshire Barnet Countryside Management Service was founded. This began as an experiment sponsored by the Countryside Commission, the Greater London Council, the London Borough of Barnet and the County Council. The service worked initially in the London Green Belt, aiming to improve land management generally, reducing trespass onto farmland while encouraging public access to the countryside, preventing the deterioration of the landscape and identifying recreational potential in the land. Amongst its early projects were planting trees and hedges in the countryside and surveys of woodland and of vegetation generally. The work of the service was progressively extended to cover the whole county and has become even more closely involved in the management of the Hertfordshire countryside, organising teams of volunteers to clear ponds, lay out new footpaths, plant trees, lay hedges and lead guided walks. Survey work has continued as well, including a recent survey of ponds in the county. The Council is also concerned with the urban landscape, and an important aspect of the department's work is in working with district planners on new town centre improvement schemes and other developments, and promoting the sympathetic improvement of historical town centres.

Another important area of concern has been in conserving the county's past. In February 1974, a County Archaeologist was appointed for the first time, working with the Planning Department. His work included the establishment of an archaeological sites and monuments record for the county and liaising with and advising local archaeological societies and district councils. In 1986, following the demise of the privately funded Hart Archaeological Unit, the Hertfordshire Archaeological Trust was set up under the auspices of the County Council, funded by both the public and private sectors. One of the most extensive excavations carried out by the Trust has been that at Chells Manor in Stevenage begun in 1988 and including the discovery of a hoard of Roman coins.

Public transport has been another aspect of the work of the Planning Department, which advises on and co-ordinates public transport throughout the county. It was largely due to Hertfordshire County Council's work that new railway stations were opened in 1982 at Watton-at-Stone and Welham Green and in 1988 at How Wood. In 1986, bus transport was de-regulated and the County Council had the task of identifying essential bus routes and issuing contracts to bus companies to cover these routes where commercial services were not provided. As well as continuing to produce area timetable booklets, a telephone enquiry service for bus and train timetables has been set up.

An important provision of the Local Government Act 1972 enabled county councils to carry out research and collect information relating to any matter concerning the county, and in Hertfordshire this opportunity has been used to the full. The 'Planis' information service monitors the economy of the county, producing regular reports on unemployment, housing and other economic matters and maintaining a register of commercial property, available to

Countryside Management: two rangers hedgelaying in the Broxbourne Woods Management Area.

commercial developers, agents and others. The department is also developing new mapping techniques involving computer technology, including digital mapping which enables cartographic data to be manipulated in numerical form. This benefits many other County Council departments since the technique enables data from different sources (not necessarily in map form) to be combined easily on a single map.

The County Council is itself a major owner of land and buildings in Hertfordshire, including schools and colleges and their grounds, residential institutions and staff housing. It also owns over 5,000 acres of agricultural land let as smallholdings together with over 4,000 acres of larger farms, woodland and other land owned to preserve the green belt around London. Most of the County Council's green belt land was bought soon after the Second World War. Since then, the amount of land it owns has remained fairly steady, though occasionally small pieces of land are disposed of (for example for road schemes) and others are acquired (the latest in 1986 when land was taken over from the former Greater London Council). Much of the land owned by the County Council is let for agricultural use, but some, though still preserved as open space, is used for other purposes: the Aldenham Golf Course and Country Club, for example, form part of the County Council's green belt estates. The County Council is possibly the largest landowner in the county, though except in the case of the farmland associated with the agricultural college at Oaklands, it does not normally farm the land itself. The new County Council, like the old, appointed a Land Agent to manage its resources, but in 1987 this department was merged with the Planning Department in order to bring together the complementary property-based skills of both departments and in order better to co-ordinate the use of the County Council's resources.

Library Service

The reorganisation of local government in 1974 affected the County Library more than most County Council services. The service expanded by almost one third, because for the first time the County Council was responsible for providing libraries throughout the whole county, including Watford, St Albans, Cheshunt and Letchworth which had previously run their own libraries (Letchworth had become a library authority in 1925, shortly after the Hertfordshire service came into existence, while Hertford Library, originally provided by the Borough of Hertford, became part of the county service in 1964). The four independent authorities did not give up their powers without a struggle; each applied to be allowed to continue to operate as an agent of the County Council, but eventually it was decided that such an arrangement would hinder the creation of a unified 'Hertfordshire Library Service' as the former 'County Library' became.

For most of its life, the Library Service has served almost exclusively the indigenous population, so that, for example, the needs of the large Italian population in Hoddesdon were almost entirely ignored in the 1950s. But in the late 1960s, the first tentative steps towards providing books in minority languages were taken when Hitchin Library began to stock books in Punjabi, and later joined the Birmingham Library Subscription Exchange scheme to provide a wider range of Punjabi books. During the 1970s and 1980s the service to minority cultures and languages has been consciously developed, so that all libraries in areas with non-English speaking populations now stock books in the relevant languages.

In the 1970s and 1980s the Library Service ceased to be a provider of books alone. It had been proposed in the early 1960s that gramophone records should be included in the service as well as books, but it was not until 1974 that records were first loaned – and then only from a few selected branches; the former independent libraries at Watford and Cheshunt had already begun to lend records. This aspect of the service has continued to grow and computer software and compact discs have now been added to the range of non-book material on offer.

'New technology' has affected not only the types of material available in libraries, but the methods of access to it and of recording loans. In 1961, equipment was installed in Welwyn Garden City Library to record loans photographically, and was so successful in speeding up book issues that the system was also introduced in other busy branches. Twenty years later, a programme was begun to record the Library Service's holdings on a computer database, and in 1982 the first libraries began to use the computer system to record issues. By 1988 over 30 libraries were using the computerised system, and in a few locations new catalogue terminals had been made available to members of the public. It is predicted that by the 1990s Hertfordshire will be operating one of the world's largest public library computer systems for circulation control, catalogue enquiries, reservations and stock ordering.

The Library Service has many aspects other than lending books in public libraries. Specialist libraries are run for schools, colleges, hospitals and in the new Bovingdon Prison, and departments of the County Council have their own technical libraries provided by the Library Service. One of the most important recent developments has been the unique Health Information Service, which provides a comprehensive information service on health and medical matters available to professionals in the National Health Service as well as to members of the public.

Museums and the Arts

It was not until the publication in 1977 of the Redcliffe-Maud Report on support for the arts in England and Wales that the County Council was persuaded to adopt a more positive attitude towards museum services and the arts. A study group was formed and a Research Assistant appointed, and in September 1979 the County Council received a report which painted a sorry picture of the state of the county's museums. One major problem was lack of resources, so that 'the evidence illustrating the history of Hertfordshire has been leaving the county at a deplorable rate during this century'.[1] Much important material – like parts of the Cassiobury collection of portraits of the Earl of Essex's family – was even in the United States. No museum specialised in the fine or decorative arts, and no museum was systematically developing a collection relating to Hertfordshire's social and industrial history. Very little archaeological field work was being carried out, and an untold amount of damage had been caused to important sites during the building of the new towns and the M1 and other roads, because museums had neither the resources nor the expertise to act. Many important archaeological collections from the county were actually held in the British Museum and elsewhere, and what did remain in Hertfordshire was inadequately looked after, since only two museums had keepers of archaeology. The collections of nearly every museum in the county were in a poor state of conservation, with no specialist staff devoted to the preservation of exhibits, and the collections were poorly documented, so that it was often impossible to use the material for the purposes of serious research. Levels of service to the public were poor; no museum had specialist display staff, and in some areas there was simply no display about the locality. In some places provision for education work was good, but in others non-existent; there was no consistency of service.

As a result of this report, a permanent Standing Committee for Museum Services in Hertfordshire was at last established, with representatives of the district councils and of the private and independent museums, as well as of the County Council. In order to carry out its work of co-ordinating, developing and promoting the work of the county's museums, a Museums Development Officer has been appointed, and one important aspect of the work has been the establishment of the Hertfordshire Heritage Fund, a charitable trust launched to assist the purchase of important pictures and artefacts for all the county's museums.

Provision for the arts at county level has taken longer to take root, though the district councils have for many years run arts centres, civic halls and other facilities for the arts. In 1984, the County Council commissioned the first Arts Development Plan for a county in the Eastern Arts region, which led to the establishment in 1985 of a Standing Committee for the Arts on similar lines to that already established for museums.

Emergency Plans

The essential work of the Emergency Planning Team is to ensure that the county as a whole is able to cope effectively with any type of emergency, whether in peace or wartime. This includes the co-ordination of local authority resources to support the Fire Brigade, Police and Ambulance services, which would need to become involved whether the emergency was a gas explosion, escape of toxic chemicals, major air crash or the result of war. An important development in emergency planning has been the establishment in 1975 under the chairmanship of the Chief Constable of the Hertfordshire Emergency Services Major Incident Committee (HESMIC) to develop a systematic approach to combined service operations in the county.

Under the Civil Defence (planning) Regulations (1974), the new county councils were made responsible for making civil defence plans. This included making plans for co-ordinating action, for providing shelters, for providing accommodation for the homeless, maintaining essential services and 'instructing and advising the public on the effects of hostile attack and on protective measures to be taken against such effects'. In 1980, the government's Defence Review decided that the country's civil defences should be updated because of what it saw as the increasingly uncertain international situation. One result of this review was the agreement to site Cruise Missiles in Britain and the other, almost equally controversial, was that once again local authorities became involved in preparing plans for civil defence in time of war. Hertfordshire's Civil Defence staff was increased from three to eight people, training courses were held and community advisors (to help the work of local government in time of war) were recruited. In 1983 the government issued a new set of civil defence regulations which required county councils to prepare detailed plans for action in the event of war. Councils also had to establish an 'emergency centre in which to control and co-ordinate action to be taken by them in the event of hostile attack or a threat of hostile attack',[2] and to train sufficient staff (including district council staff) to enable the plans to be carried out effectively. In 1987, the government introduced the concept of civil protection which suggested that local authorities should plan for peacetime and wartime emergencies together, to provide an 'all-hazards' plan co-ordinating all aspects of civil defence.

Training is an important aspect of the work of the department, both for individual services and to ensure efficient co-operation. A major HESMIC training event is held about once a year, with smaller scale exercises more frequently. The A1(M) Hatfield Tunnel was used before it opened to simulate a multiple motorway crash, which was particularly difficult to cope with in the confines of the tunnel. Another exercise, held at the County Council's premises at Goldings and involving over 800 people working in the fields of communications, first aid, feeding, policing and rest centre management, simulated the type of aid and assistance which would be needed from a variety of voluntary organisations in the event of any major incident.

Environmental Services

The Environmental Services Department was created in 1974 as the successor to the Public Health section of the former County Health Department, after most of that department's duties passed to the Area Health Authorities. It operates in two main areas. First, it advises on environmental health and hygiene in the County Council's own establishments, including its many schools. This includes regular testing of the 180 school swimming pools and inspection of school kitchens, as well as investigating specific problems such as those caused on one occasion by the release of low levels of formaldehyde from the chipboard used to construct portable classrooms.

Another aspect of the section's work is concerned with the regulation of waste disposal facilities, including hazardous waste. Waste disposal sites have to be licensed under the Control of Pollution Act 1974. Waste disposal can cause problems ranging from the short term, such as litter and mud being carried on to public roads, to long-term issues such as flammable gas and leachate (polluting liquid) from decomposing waste. Licences include conditions designed to control these problems. Breaches of licence conditions or use of unlicenced facilities can lead to prosecution – for example a Watford pharmacist was taken to court over shop waste including drugs which was dumped on open land in the centre of the town.

Trading Standards

In 1974, the former Weights and Measures Department was renamed 'Trading Standards', but the verification of weights and measures remained an important aspect of its work. Methods of working had remained unchanged for many years, but the 1970s saw a number of new developments, beginning with the introduction of metrication. The compulsory use of metric weights and measures began with pharmaceuticals in 1971; it was originally intended that the process of metrication would be complete by 1975, but time has shown this hope to have been unjustified. A major change took place in 1980. Up to that time, the stated contents of packaged goods were minimum weights or quantities. Because of EEC requirements, these were now replaced by the use of average measurements, and this naturally required considerable adjustments to the department's methods of verification. Instead of testing individual packaged goods in retail shops, batches of packages would be taken for statistical sampling at factories; emphasis has shifted from detecting short weight in shops to preventing it in factories. This change was justified because packing machinery can now be mass-produced to extremely high standards of accuracy. Individual items of equipment are still tested on traders' premises, but despite the complexity of modern equipment, only about 10 per cent of those tested in 1987 were found to be inaccurate. The principle of providing reassurance to consumers that they are receiving the quantities stated by the trader or his measuring equipment have not changed – though the methods (such as the use of dummy petrol tanks in cars in order to detect short measures from petrol pumps) are often very different from those a hundred years ago.

The work of examination and sampling of food continues to be an aspect of the department's work, but the impurities revealed today tend to be the result of accidental contamination by foreign bodies (such as snails in packets of frozen peas, slugs, larvae or foil in milk or string, metal, glass in bread) rather than the deliberate adulteration common in the early twentieth century. The correct labelling of packaged goods, especially food, has become increasingly important during the last few decades, and all Trading Standards departments seek to ensure that labelling is accurate and not misleading. A development of the 1980s, important both in this respect and for other aspects of consumer protection, has been the 'Home Authority Concept', by which each authority accepts responsibility for the observance of consumer protection law by the manufacturers, importers and packers within its area who produce goods for national distribution. In Hertfordshire, for example, these include Tesco, Mothercare and Nabisco.

Consumer protection as it is understood today did not really begin until the late 1960s. Under the Consumer Protection Act 1961 (extended under later legislation), the Secretary of State was given the power to make regulations concerning the safety of products, making it possible to give the public much more effective protection, particularly from new or newly identified dangers. Regulations were made about a wide variety of products, such as hood cords in children's coats and other clothing (which were banned in 1976) or the safety of toys. The Trade Descriptions Act 1968 was another important piece of consumer protection legislation enforced by the department: false descriptions of goods, false indications of price and misleading statements about goods and services became illegal. With the increasing interest in consumer protection and the publicity afforded to the subject in the press and on television, the department became increasingly involved in giving advice and investigating complaints from members of the public and in the 1970s, Consumer Affairs Officers were appointed for the first time, to help and advise the public.

The department's new role was reflected in the name it adopted in 1974, when the old Weights and Measures Department became the Trading Standards Department. The name 'Consumer Protection Department' adopted in some counties, was, however, rejected. A report to the County Council pointed out 'As a title, "Consumer Protection" is attractively topical, but this is unacceptable because it indicates a bias towards the consumer and does not reflect the Department's impartiality – much of the Inspectorate's time and expertise is devoted to advising and assisting retail traders, manufacturers and packers,' [3] In 1974, the Watford Borough Council opened Hertfordshire's first Consumer Advice Centre, and Trading Standards Department staff visited both it and the county's eighteen Citizens Advice Bureaux to provide consumer advice. Now, thousands of complaints are received every year, and the field of consumer protection – both in its safety and its trade descriptions aspects – probably provides the widest variety of work for trading standards officers. During the 1980's, problems with second-hand cars, and particularly 'clocking' or adjusting of mileometers to give false readings, have grown especially fast. Other matters on which much time has been spent have been the sale of counterfeit goods, which are generally imported, poor quality goods ranging from sports clothing to car components which bear the brand-name of trusted British companies. The sale of unsafe goods too has given much cause for concern such as the potentially lethal light bulbs which, due to a manufacturing fault had a piece of wire protruding from the metal base. The department is no longer concerned with goods alone but also with services, including holiday packages, consumer credit and especially secured loans.

County Record Office

The most noticeable effect in Hertfordshire of the 1974 reorganisation of local government was probably the replacement of the old urban and rural district councils by the new, larger, district councils. Under the 1972 Local Government Act the Record Office has the duty of preserving and making available for study records of the abolished urban and rural district councils, which has made considerable demands on Record Office accommodation and staff time. In 1988, these records occupied about 500 metres of shelving, and more are still being received as they cease to be in current use by the successor district councils.

The care of the records created and owned by the Hertfordshire County Council, which were the original reason for the Record Office's creation have over the years become just one aspect of its work. By 1988, around 670 metres of its shelving carried the records of the County Council and its predecessors such as the School Boards, whose functions and hence whose records it has inherited. This is only about one-fifth of the total of around 3,700 metres (over 2 miles) of records held. However, County Council records have never ceased to be a major concern of the Record Office, and in particular, efforts have been made to ensure that the needs of future historians of the County Council, as well as its own future administrative needs, will be met. As early as 1955, the County Archivist drew up guidelines agreed with each department for the transfer of records to the Record Office; unfortunately these seem to have been poorly observed by many departments, and as it has never been possible – nor desirable – for Record Office staff to monitor departmental records, the preservation of such records is likely to be inconsistent. A new initiative to deal with the ever increasing problem of departmental records started in 1972 when a records management programme was begun. A records centre was established to provide cheap and compact storage for records no longer in everyday use; the County Council's essential archival records can be identified and earmarked for preservation at an early stage, while unwanted records can be destroyed systematically instead of taking up valuable storage space for longer than necessary.

The main function of the Record Office has always been to preserve the county's records for future generations, which it does by storing them in a secure and controlled physical environment, by repairing professionally the most fragile items and by listing and identifying them. It has also made the records available for study, and over the last 30 years or so, in common with all local government record offices, this public face of the work has taken more and more of the available resources. This is largely because of the enormous growth of interest in local history and particularly family history, coupled with the post-war increase in available leisure time and resources for travelling. During 1935, only fifteen visits to the record room were recorded (including two by the

Top; *A visitor to the County Record Office researches an aspect of the county's history.* Bottom; *One of the many documents illustrating the history of the county now housed securely in the County Record Office.*

prominent Hitchin local historian Reginald Hine). In 1953, searchers made 121 visits to the Record Office; by 1972 this had grown to 1,650, and by 1988 to nearly 4,000 visits. Numbers of enquiries by post and telephone for information from the records held have also risen by a comparable degree. The type of research carried out by visitors to the office has changed, too. In the past, the typical searcher was the professional or experienced amateur historian who required guidance only to identify the records he required. Today, the typical visitor may never previously have used or even seen original historical records. Each visit therefore involves a high proportion of contact with professional staff (whose numbers are at a similar level to that of the 1960s), who have therefore found less and less time for other duties.

Architecture

By the 1960s, the County Architect's Department included quantity surveyors, land and building surveyors and structural, heating and electrical engineers as well as architects so that most types of building and maintenance work could be carried out 'in-house'. By the early 1970s the department had a strength of 300 people, but it was one of the victims of the financial stringencies of the time which forced cuts of around a third of this number. A critical backlog in maintenance work developed, and the situation did not improve until more money began to be available in the mid-1980s.

Building did not, of course, cease altogether during this period – one notable project of the time was the new building at County Hall itself (1976). Already by the 1940s, the attic and basement floors of County Hall, originally intended for storage, were being used for office accommodation, and by the 1950s a great deal of temporary hutting was also being used for offices. By the 1960s it was evident that the extensions to the building envisaged on the original plans could not be long delayed. For a while, an enormous tower block (on a site which is already the highest point in the locality) was considered but fortunately the extensions completed in 1976 are on a much more human scale. Unlike the original buildings, the extensions were designed by the County Architect's Department. There was considerable discussion about the introduction of open-plan offices in the new building, but with the number of staff to be accommodated and the need to be as flexible as possible, this was the arrangement eventually adopted. Despite the new building, the shortage of office space is still acute, and plans are now at an early stage to provide additional accommodation.

Since SEAC was wound up in 1977, traditional building methods have generally been used for schools and other buildings. In common with most domestic and commercial building of the last decade, brick and timber have replaced metal, concrete and large areas of glass. The design of many new buildings, too, has resembled domestic work, particularly in buildings for the Social Services Department. Large homes for children, old people or the handicapped are being replaced by small houses; and corridors, shared bedrooms and communal facilities by private bedsitting rooms on a domestic scale. In Scarborough House, Stevenage (1976–1978), for example, a home for the mentally handicapped, each resident has a bed-sitting room in one of the three 'bungalows', each housing just eight people. Instead of being provided with communal meals, the residents prepare their own meals in the kitchen provided in each bungalow.

A typical example of 'post-SEAC' work is the new library at Abbots Langley (1980–1981), with its corner windows, red brick walls and slate and timber roof. One consideration in the design of this library was the use of materials and a design which would harmonise with the adjacent church. An increased sensitivity to the role of historic buildings in the landscape has been characteristic of the period since the mid-1970s. This has also been expressed in the restoration work carried out on the Council's older buildings. Throughout its existence the County Council has used older buildings, many – such as the Shire Hall in Hertford, Wall Hall, Bayfordbury, Balls Park, Hadham Hall and Hitchin Priory – of some historical and architectural importance. Until recently, however, adaptation of these for modern use has tended to be utilitarian, with the age and associations of the building seen as an impediment to its new use rather than as something to be exploited. Such buildings are often expensive to maintain and inappropriate to the smaller, more domestic scale of building required today, particularly by the Social Services Department, and many have now been sold. But some remain, particularly in educational use, and several have been subject to restoration. In 1974, the County Council won a Civic Trust Award for its restoration of a fourteenth-century tithe barn at St Joan of Arc School, Rickmansworth; not simply an 'adaptation', but an attempt to restore the fourteenth-century appearance as far as possible. The largest project of this type to be undertaken, estimated to cost almost £2 million, is the restoration of the Shire Hall at Hertford, built in 1768 by James Adam, and used as a court house ever since. This desire to preserve and re-create the past is, of course, part of a general late-twentieth century concern, manifesting itself in many other fields as well as architecture.

Corporate Concerns

In 1972, before the Local Government Bill had even become law, the County Council's working report on plans for the future, *The New County Council*, asserted that one essential job of the new Council would be to build a 'corporate identity [which] is one way of establishing "togetherness" in Local Authority staff and protecting a corporate image outwards to the ratepayer'. The same document, most significantly, likened the County Council, with its then 40,000 staff, to a large industrial concern which must be run efficiently – an image which would have occurred to few in the days when local government tended to be seen as an unstructured conglomerate of different departments, each with different and often incompatible needs. Since 1974, this corporate image has been consciously developed and the County Council's resemblance to a commercial organisation has become more apparent.

The Bains Report had emphasised the importance of a corporate structure and management at both member and officer level. It advocated the establishment of Policy Committees to determine overall direction and the allocation of resources. This suggestion was not at first adopted in Hertfordshire, though the new Finance and Resources Committee was a step in this direction. In 1986, though, a Policy and Resources Committee was established, which absorbed the work of the Co-ordinating and General Purposes Committee and the Personnel and Support Services Committee.

The importance of a corporate structure was reflected in the internal administrative arrangements of the new council. As well as a single Chief Executive at the head of the administrative structure, a Chief Officers' Management Team was established as a forum for departmental heads to co-ordinate their work. Resources, too, were increasingly managed as a whole. In 1974, for example, the Fire and Ambulance Brigade workshop and the Highways Department workshop, which each maintained the vehicles of just one department, merged to form a single workshop to maintain all the Council's vehicles.

The County Council has, since 1974, increasingly ceased to rely solely on its internal resources, but has used the expert services of outside organisations. The Social Services Department, for example, works with MIND (the organisation for the mentally ill) and MENCAP (for the mentally handicapped). The Women's Royal Voluntary Service and other volunteer organisations figure largely in the Emergency Planning Team's plans for a major disaster. Most significant in this field has been liaison with industry, particularly in education, with work-experience placements, commercial input into curriculum planning and industrial representatives on college governing bodies and advisory committees. This liaison has been if anything even stronger in the opposite direction, with the County Council giving (and increasingly selling) its expertise to industry and commerce. The County Library's Commercial Information Service, for example (based at Hatfield Polytechnic and managed and funded jointly with HERTIS) provides a comprehensive information service to commerce and industry. The Trading Standards Department, which has probably been serving industrial and commercial concerns for longer than any other department, has been developing its advisory service to industry. The Council sells goods as well as services; since 1974 Hertfordshire County Supplies (which supplies equipment to schools and other Council organisations) has served Suffolk, Bedfordshire and the London Borough of Harrow as well as Hertfordshire, and the service is soon to be extended to the London Borough of Enfield.

The Council tries to offer 'value for money' to its customers – the public – and must be seen to be doing so. Since 1889, the Council has been answerable to the ratepayers for the services offered, and except perhaps in the period of expansion following the Second World War, has been extremely cost-conscious. With the continuing reduction, and eventual loss of the rate support grant, this has become even more necessary. Making the best use of what resources remain is now, however, being seen as a positive virtue. The County Council regularly compares its performance with that of similar local authorities. It consults its public over many aspects of its work. Consultation was especially extensive in the case of the County Structure Plan, but most other departments have been involved to some extent. The Social Services Department, for example, produced their 'Tomorrow's Services' proposals on the care of people with a mental handicap jointly with the Regional Health Authority.

For a number of years, the Council has issued a brief leaflet to ratepayers explaining how their money is spent, but in 1987 the county's first *Annual Review* was published. In it, each County Council department provides a report of its work during the previous year, both for staff in other parts of the vast organisation and, as Frank Cogan (Chairman 1984–1987) said, for 'the million or so people in Hertfordshire who are the Council's customers and to whom we are all accountable'.[5]

At school at the turn of the century ... and now.

6

Contrasts
1889–1989

During the last 100 years, the county of Hertfordshire has changed enormously, but not so greatly that the proverbial time traveller would not be able to recognise it. The boundaries today are not very different from those of 1889; the major change has been the loss of Barnet and East Barnet and the gain of Potters Bar, formerly in Middlesex, which took place in 1965. Many of the county's famous buildings, as different as Hatfield House and St Albans Cathedral, still stand, though perhaps in better shape than at the end of the nineteenth century; many of the most attractive villages like Ashwell and Westmill still retain their charm. Most of the changes in the county are a result of the enormous growth of population it has experienced: from 220,000 residents in 1889 to nearly a million today. Towns have grown, and there have been two brand-new garden cities and four new towns (Welwyn Garden City was a new town as well as a garden city), which at their peak growth in the 1960s housed a fifth of the county's population. Patterns of work and leisure have altered, and with the advent of the motor car, transport has become very different from the days when railways reigned, though it is still, despite the advent of the M25, easier to cross the county from north to south than from east to west.

The County Council of today is still an elected body of councillors, but there are no longer County Aldermen chosen by the members themselves; all the members are elected by the people of Hertfordshire, and unlike the early days when the payment of rates was the primary qualification for voting, today almost every Hertfordshire resident over the age of eighteen has the right to elect a County Councillor. The elected members today work much harder than their counterparts in 1889 and although there is far too much business for them to involve themselves in the trivial and routine matters the 1889 councillors discussed, they are probably better informed about the wider issues of local government generally. Unlike the members of the first Council, who were typically local gentry and squires who belonged to a number of local boards, committees and authorities, today's councillors are more single-minded in their commitment to the County Council, and are more likely to be business men and women, public servants or retired industrialists than landowners. National politics were never considered in the early Council elections, but today it is assumed that electors will vote for a political party rather than just for an individual, and as a result, every member was elected in 1985 on a party political basis. The electorate has changed, too. Even if its turnout for elections may be no higher, there is an intense and informed interest in the County Council's services as they affect individuals. In such areas as education, transportation and the environment, members of the public are articulate and their expectations are high. They want not just to be consulted but for their preferences to be met.

The County Council's powers and duties today are far greater than those of the first Council. It ran the Hertfordshire Police Force then as now, and as today, administrative difficulties occurred in the southern part of the county which is in the Metropolitan Police District. It has also retained responsibility for weights and measures. In 1889 it was responsible for just a few of the county's roads, most not yet tarred, and only a tenth of the length of those it builds and repairs today. The County Council's lunatic asylum at Arlesey is now a National Health Service hospital, and during its life the Council was to gain and then to lose responsibility for many other hospitals. Most of its other duties in 1889 were minor. Most important of all the Council's new powers has been the acquisition of reponsibility for education. Not one of the many schools and colleges the County Council runs today was its responsibility in 1889, and very few of today's school buildings existed at all. It has also gained responsibility for (in chronological order) archives, planning, libraries, social services and the Fire Brigade, and has developed a flourishing Architect's Department.

Financial growth has been on an enormous scale. In the early years the Council spent about £106,000 a year, which is only about 0.03 per cent of today's expenditure, and most of that money came directly from local rates or from 'assigned revenues', which could vary in amount from year to year. Today finance is again a problem, as during the last few years the county has received less and less support from the government, and once again local rates are the main source of income. Today, the Council spends around £600m every year, a large proportion of which goes on staff salaries, and almost half of which goes towards education.

Perhaps the biggest contrast with the nineteenth-century Council is in the matter of staff. Instead of a few part-time officers, very few of whom were directly responsible to the County Council, there is now a largely full-time staff, representing many different professions and skills, and which is almost a fifth of the size of the total population of the county in 1889! There are now staff associations, a staff restaurant at County Hall, and many of the Council's employees are members of the National and Local Government Officers Association (founded in 1905), or other unions, all of which would have been unthinkable in 1889. Also surprising to the nineteenth-century councillors would have been the number of women on the County Council's staff. Women teachers were not unusual even in the nineteenth century, but even in their case advertisements would have specified the sex, and often the age of the person required. Today it is not only County Council policy to make all jobs open equally to men and to women (and to members of all the other so-called 'minority' groups), but it would be illegal for it to do otherwise.

The early County Council had no permanent home. It met alternately in Hertford and St Albans, its committee meetings were held in London and its offices were scattered throughout Hertfordshire and London. Today it has a permanent home at County Hall, opened during the year of its 50th birthday. The presence of central offices has enabled a cohesion of the Council's services to occur to a degree which would have been impossible in 1889. The great majority of the County Council's staff are, however, out in the county, serving its people from more than 1,000 premises – old people's and children's homes; hostels and day centres; divisional and local offices and depots; and schools, colleges and libraries.

One final contrast. The first County Council made little ceremony about its first meeting. It did not particularly wish to advertise its existence and saw its main purpose as providing the minimum of essential services as economically and unobtrusively as possible. By 1918, the Council was sufficiently ebullient to permit the clerk to record in the minutes the singing of the National Anthem on Armistice Day. By 1939, when it celebrated its 50th anniversary, it celebrated with a dinner for past and present councillors at Hatfield House and a souvenir programme. The ordinary ratepayers of Hertfordshire were not included in the celebrations, though admittedly the Second World War was about to begin. In 1989, in contrast, when it celebrates its centenary, the Council has become well aware of the potential and importance of public relations, and the desirability of promoting its public image, as well as the need to be accountable to the people of Hertfordshire whom it serves. The Hertfordshire County Council is involving not only a great number of its staff, but members of the public as well, with exhibitions, open days and concerts, as well as this history, all in celebration of the hundredth birthday of the Hertfordshire County Council.

Appendix 1

CHAIRMEN OF THE COUNTY COUNCIL

The County Council's first Chairman, Francis Thomas de Grey, the seventh Earl Cowper.

The Old County Council, 1889 – 1974

The Earl Cowper, KG	1889 – 1901
Sir John Evans, KCB, DCL, FRS	1901 – 1905
Rt Hon Sir Thomas Frederick Halsey, Bt	1905 – 1920
Sir Edmund Broughton Barnard, DL, OBE	1920 – 1930
Sir Joseph Child Priestley, KC	1930 – 1939
Sir David Carter Rutherford, DL	1939 – 1946
Rev Roland Smith	1946
Sir Harold Herbert Williams FBA, FSA	1947 – 1952

Brig Sir Edward H L Beddington, DL, CMG, DSO, MC   1952 – 1958
E J Baxter, OBE   1958 – 1961
Sir John Cockram, FCA   1961 – 1965
Claude C Barker, LLB, CBE   1965 – 1969
Dame Betty Paterson   1969 – 1973
Major A J Hughes, MC, TD, DL   1973 – 1974

The County Council's present Chairman, Fred Peacock.

The New County Council, 1973 –

Philip Ireton, DL   1973 – 1977
Major A J Hughes, MC, TD   1977 – 1980
W A Hill, OBE   1980 – 1982
S C Purkiss   1982 – 1984
Frank Cogan   1984 – 1987
Fred Peacock, JP, FRSA   1987 –

Appendix 2

CHIEF OFFICERS OF THE COUNTY COUNCIL

The Old County Council, 1889 – 1974

Clerk

Sir Richard Nicholson [Clerk of the Peace 1865]	1889 – 1894
Sir Charles Elton Longmore, KCB	1894 – 1930
Philip Elton Longmore, CBE	1930 – 1948
(Arthur) Neville Moon	1948 – 1969
Frederick Peter Boyce, CBE	1969 – 1974

County Accountant

William Brock Keen	1889 – 1939
Richard Sedgwick McDougall	1939 – 1949
[combined with County Treasurer 1949 – see below]	

County Treasurer

Sir Charles Elton Longmore, KCB [served from 1879]	1889 – 1894
Peter Williamson Dumville	1894 – 1900
[Barclays Bank Ltd]	1900 – 1949
Richard Sedgwick McDougall, CBE	1949 – 1957
John Cooper Alexander	1957 – 1972
Cyril Charles Jasper	1972 – 1974

County Finance Officer
[became Chief Cashier within Treasurer's Department 1939]

F Hibbert	1899 – 1913
V M Spencer	1913 – 1939

County Surveyor

Urban Armstrong Smith [served from 1876]	1889 – 1914
John Spencer Killick	1914 – 1920
Albert Ernest Prescott, DSO	1920 – 1946
Charles Henry ffoliott	1946 – 1962
John Vernon Leigh, MBE	1962 – 1971
Michael F Hardy, OBE	1971 – 1974

Chief Constable

Henry S Daniell [served from 1880]	1889 – 1911
Alfred Letchworth Law	1911 – 1928
George T Knight, MBE	1928 – 1939
S M E Fairburn	1939 – 1945
Arthur Edwin Young	1945 – 1947
Albert Frederick Wilcox, CBE	1947 – 1969
Raymond Naylor Buxton, OBE, BEM	1969 – 1974

County Medical Officer

John Andrew Turner	1897 – 1900
Robert Ayton Dunn	1901 – 1902
Francis E Fremantle	1902 – 1916
Henry Hyslop Thompson	1916 – 1940
James Liddell Dunlop	1940 – 1962
Geoffrey Wilfred Knight	1962 – 1974

County Education Officer
[Until 1941, Chief Education Officer, in Clerk's Department]

Archibald S Hallidie	1903 – 1926
Samuel W Howe	1926 – 1940
Sir John Hubert Newsom, CBE	1940 – 1957
Sidney Thomas Broad, CBE	1957 – 1974

County Land Agent

George John Turner	1919 – 1941
Frederick Charles Burgess	1942 – 1951
Ernest Marsden Mitchell	1951 – 1955
Donald George Merriott	1955 – 1974

County Librarian
[In Education Department until 1965]

William Pickard	1925 – 1935
T W Muskett	1935 – 1947
M F Austin (Mrs Thwaite)	1948 – 1952
Lorna Paulin, OBE	1952 – 1974

Civil Defence and Road Safety Officer

Joseph Edmonds Slattery, MBE	1937 – 1964
John Edwards	1964 – 1968
Idwal Griffiths Roberts	1968 – 1974

County Architect

Charles Herbert Aslin, CBE	1945 – 1958
Geoffrey Charles Fardell, CBE	1958 – 1973
Jack Leonard Stanford Digby	1973 – 1974

County Archivist
[County Records Officer until 1950]

William Le Hardy, MC	1946 – 1961
Peter Walne	1962 – 1974

County Planning Officer

Ernest Henry Doubleday, OBE	1947 – 1968
Lawrence Charles Kitching, MBE	1968 – 1972
David Overton	1972 – 1974

Chief Fire and Ambulance Officer

Geoffrey Vaughan Blackstone, CBE, GM	1947 – 1971
James Maul Flemming, MBE	1971 – 1974

Children's Officer

Sylvia Watson, OBE	1948 – 1971

County Welfare Officer

Wilfred Henry Finch	1948 – 1964
Ronald Stanley James Potter	1964 – 1970

Director of Social Services

James Bainbridge Chaplin, CBE	1971 – 1974

The New County Council 1974 –

Chief Executive

Peter Boyce	1974 – 1979
Morris le Fleming	1979 –

County Secretary

Morris le Fleming	1974 – 1979
William J Church	1979 –

County Treasurer

Cyril Jasper	1974 – 1982
Kenneth S Cliff	1982 –

County Surveyor

Michael F Hardy, OBE	1974 – 1988
Nigel Knott	1988 –

Chief Constable

Raymond Naylor Buxton, OBE, BEM	1974 – 1977
Adrian Fraser Canning Clissitt	1977 – 1984
Trefor A Morris	1984 –

Chief Fire Officer

James Maul Flemming, MBE	1974 – 1977
Edward S Faulkner	1977 –

County Architect

Jack Digby	1974 – 1977
John Onslow	1977 –

County Land Agent
[Merged with Planning Department 1986; see County Planning and Estates Officer]

R A Buckley	1974 – 1978
B S Garrett	1978 –

County Planning and Estates Officer
[County Planning Officer until 1987]

David Overton	1974 – 1978
Geoffrey Steeley	1978 –

County Education Officer

Donald Fisher, CBE	1974 –

Director of Social Services

James Bainbridge Chaplin, CBE	1974 – 1975
Herbert Laming, CBE	1975 –

County Librarian

Lorna Paulin, OBE	1974 – 1976
E M (Max) Broome, OBE	1976 –

County Archivist

Peter Walne	1974 –

County Trading Standards Officer*

Ian Welch	1974 – 1987
Nicholas Cull	1987 –

County Environmental Services Officer*

Jack Stringer 1974 – 1983
Malcolm Allen 1983 –

County Emergency Plans Officer*

Idwal Griffiths Roberts 1974 – 1984
David Moses 1984 –

County Personnel Officer*

Kenneth Gamston 1974 –

*The County Trading Standards, Environmental Services, Emergency Plans and Personnel Officers are all within the County Secretary's Department

Bibliography

References prefixed HRO are to records held in the Hertfordshire Record Office. HCC without the prefix HRO indicates an item published by the County Council.
Many of the published items are also held in the County Record Office Library. The place of publication of books is London unless stated otherwise.

GENERAL BACKGROUND

Marwick, Arthur, *The Explosion of British Society 1914–1970* (1971)
Marwick, Arthur, *British Society Since 1945* (1982)
Stevenson, John, *British Society 1914–1945* (1984)
Lloyd, T O, *Empire to Welfare State, 1906–1985* (Oxford, 1986)
Various editors, *Annual Review* for the years 1888–1987

LOCAL GOVERNMENT GENERALLY

Keith-Lucas, Bryan and Richards, Peter G, *A History of Local Government in the Twentieth Century* (1978)
Radcliffe, C W, *Middlesex: The Jubilee of the County Council 1889–1939* (1939)
Le Hardy, William (ed), *Guide to the Hertfordshire Record Office part I* (HCC 1961)

HERTFORDSHIRE COUNTY COUNCIL

The primary source throughout has been the minutes of the County Council and of its various committees and sub-committees, Annual Budgets and Accounts, together with the annual or other reports of Chief Officers, where these are not included in the series of minutes (HRO, HCC [pre 1974 County Council] and 2HCC [new County Council]).

Information particularly for the more recent period supplied by Chief Officers and other officers of the Council.

Hertfordshire County Council Annual Review 1986/87 and 1987/88 (HCC)

The *Hertfordshire Mercury* (file copies in HRO) has provided occasional details not available from the offical sources.
Cooper, D 'Hertfordshire County Council 1889–1974' [a manuscript history held in the Record Office which, however, concentrates heavily on the committee and departmental structure and the legal basis for the County Council's work, rather than the services it has provided, which I have made the subject of the current account].

COUNTY COUNCIL SERVICES

Architecture

Bird, Eric L, 'The Post-War Schools of the Hertfordshire County Council', *Journal of the Royal Institute of British Architects*, September 1949 (HRO HEd 3/25)
Hertfordshire County Council Builds: 1935–1984 (HCC)
Maclure, S, *Educational Development and School Building 1945–1973* (1984)
[see also references under 'Education']

Education

Society of Archivists, *The Records of Education Departments: Their Retention and Management* (Society of Archivists, 1987) [for the statutory background to educational developments]
Barnard, H C, *A History of English Education from 1760* (1964)
Hertfordshire – New Schools for Old (1950)
A Hundred New Schools – School Building 1948–1954 (HCC 1954)
Education in Hertfordshire (HCC 1957) (HRO HEd 3/26)
Secondary Education in Hertfordshire (HCC 1978)
Parker, D H 'The impact of the First World War upon Elementary Education in Hertfordshire' (unpublished thesis, 1987)
Historical introductions to HRO catalogues of Education Department Records (including records of schools and other institutions *HRO* HEd)
[see also references under 'Architecture']

Fire Service

Annual Reports of the Hertfordshire Fire Brigade
Preston, 'Fire Service in Watford' *Journal of Watford and District Industrial History Society* No 2 1972

Health and Welfare

Annual Reports of the Medical Officer of Health, 1897–1973 (HRO HSS)
Stroud, John, *The Shorn Lamb* (1960) [a novel about children in care, based on his experience as a Children's Officer in Hertfordshire]

Highways

Road Accident and Casualty Statistics, Hertfordshire, 1987 (HCC)

Library Service

County Librarian's Annual Reports 1928–1948 (HRO off acc 587)
Ashby, Margaret, *Hertis: The development of a Library Network* (Hatfield 1986)

Planning

Osborn, F and Whittick, A, *The New Towns: The Answer to Megalopolis* (1963)
Davidge, W R, *Hertfordshire Regional Planning Report, 1927* (HCC 1927)
Hertfordshire: Survey Report and Analysis of County Development Plan (HCC 1951)

Police

Annual Reports of the Hertfordshire Constabulary 1970 to date
Minutes of the Standing Joint Committee (HRO HJC)
Osborn, Neil, *The Story of Hertfordshire Police* (Herts Countryside 1969)

Record Office

Ed, William Le Hardy, *Guide to the Hertfordshire Record Office part I* (HCC 1961)
Annual Reports of the County Archivist, 1953 to date
Record Room Visitors' book, 1932–1953 (HRO CC Misc 14)
Minutes of Quarter Sessions, 1835 (HRO QSB 21 [p 225])
Schedule of records held in the Shire Hall, 1825 (HRO CC Misc 15)

Social Services

[see references under 'Health and Welfare']

Town and Country Planning

[see references under 'Planning']

Trading Standards

O'Keefe's Weights and Measures, issue 19
Annual Reports of the Trading Standards Officer 1979 to date

Welfare

[see references under 'Health and Welfare']

REFERENCES

All references are to items held in the Hertfordshire Record Office. Record Office Catalogue references, where appropriate, are given in parentheses.

Chapter 2

1 *Hertfordshire Mercury*, 12 January 1898
2 Minutes of Hertfordshire County Council (HCC 1/1)
3 Minutes of County Buildings Committee (HCC 8/1)
4 Minutes of Highways Committee (HCC 6/19)
5 Minutes of Highways Committee (HCC 6/21)
6 Register of Vehicles Licensed 1903 – 1910
7 William Le Hardy, ed., *Guide to the Hertfordshire Record Office part 1*
8 Schedule of deeds and papers in the county cupboards at the Shire Hall (CC Misc 15 – 17)
9 Minutes of Highways Committee (HCC 6/5)
10 Minutes of Records Committee (HCC 18/1)
11 William Le Hardy, ed.,*Guide to the Hertfordshire Record Office part 1*
12 Annual Report of County Medical Officer of Health, 1901 (HSS)
13 Annual Report of County Medical Officer of Health, 1905 (HSS)
14 Annual Report of County Medical Officer of Health, 1911 (HSS)
15 Annual Report of County Medical Officer of Health (Report of Inspector of Midwives), 1906 (HSS)
16 Minutes of Central School Attendance Committee (HCC 21F/4)
17 Minutes of Hertfordshire War Agricultural Committee (AEC 1)
18 Minutes of Hertfordshire County Council (HCC 1/38)

Chapter 3

1 Minutes of Education Committee (HCC 21/13)
2 Minutes of Hertfordshire County Council (HCC 1/56)
3 Hertfordshire County Council Papers Issued (HCC 2/128)
4 Robert Woodhouse, 'Being Plainly Told'
5 Sir Edward Beddington, 'My Life' (D/EX 205 F1)
6 Annual Reports of Chief Education Officer (HEd 3/7/1)
7 Minutes of Mental Deficiency Act Committee (HCC 30/1). [The Act itself, 3 & 4 George 5, ch28, uses slightly different terms]
8 Annual Report of County Medical Officer of Health (Report under Mental Deficiency Act 1913), 1919 (HSS)
9 Annual Report of County Medical Officer of Health, 1919 (HSS)
10 Minutes of Cottage Homes Sub-committee of St Albans Board of Guardians (HSS)

11 Minutes of Vagrancy Sub-committee of Public Assistance Committee (HCC 37M/1)
12 Ibid
13 Minutes of Public Assistance Committee (HCC 37/3)
14 Davidge, W R, *Hertfordshire Regional Planning Report, 1927*
15 Ibid
16 Minutes of Central Organisation Committee (HCC 41/1)
17 Minutes of Finance and General Purposes Committee (HCC 7/29)
18 *Hertfordshire Mercury*, 8 November 1935
19 Minutes of Emergency Committee (HCC 45/1)
20 Minutes of Finance and General Purposes Sub-committee of Education Committee (HCC 21D/36)
21 Minutes of Physical Training and Practical Instruction Sub-committee of Education Committee (HCC 21M/5)
22 Minutes of Finance and General Purposes Sub-committee of Education Committee (HCC 21D/35)

Chapter 4

1 Annual Report of County Medical Officer of Health on School Health, 1950–1951 [presented 1952] (HCC 2/212)
2 Hertfordshire County Council War Plan (UDC 11/106)
3 Minutes of Ambulance Sub-committee of Health Committee (HCC 48/2)
4 Minutes of Highways Committee (HCC 6/69)
5 Library Sub-committee of Education Committee (HCC 21O/5)

Chapter 5

1 Minutes of Cultural and Recreational Facilities Committee (2HCC 6/2)
2 Civil Defence (General Local Authority Functions) Regulations 1983
3 Hertfordshire County Council Background Note: Trading Standards Department
4 *The New County Council* Volume 1: November 1972; Volume 2; March 1973
5 *Hertfordshire County Council: Annual Review 1986/87*

Index

Abbots Langley 14, 107
Abercrombie, Sir Patrick 64
Adam, James 24, 48, 107
Agriculture 7, 13, 27, 29-30, 96, 98
Aldbury 53
Aldenham 99; Wall Hall 65, 72, 85-6, 107
Arlesey (Bedfordshire): Fairfield hospital 10, 16, 25, 112
Ashwell 27, 73, 111
Aslin, Charles 56, 75
Atkinson, Robert 48
Austin, Mary 67

Baldock 9, 14, 85
Barnard, Sir Edmund 33
Barnet 9, 40, 44, 56, 72, 74, 96, 111; East 9, 24, 56, 111; New 75
Beddington, Sir Edward 33-4
Bedfordshire 10, 16, 24, 25, 95, 108
Benington 59
Berkhamstead 9, 13, 40, 66, 70
Bishops Stortford 9, 13, 40, 65, 69, 71, 74, 92
Blackstone, Geoffrey 58
Borehamwood 64, 70, 73
Bovingdon 36, 99
Boyce, Peter 82
Brookmans Park 62
Broxbourne 70
Buckinghamshire 40, 79
Building and architecture 16, 17, 46, 48, 56, 69, 75-7, 90, 98, 106-7, 112
Buntingford 70, 92
Bushey 19, 38, 59, 66, 67, 73
Butler, R A (Minister of Education) 68, 75

Cambridge/Cambridgeshire 40, 79
Carpenders Park 73
Cassiobury 100
Cell Barnes 38, 88
Chelsea College of Technology 72
Cheshire 21, 98
Cheshunt 9, 28, 36, 40, 75, 98, 99
Chorleywood 44
Civil Defence and emergency planning 50-52, 57-8, 59, 83, 93, 100-101, 108
Clerk of the Peace/of the County Council 11, 17, 19, 24, 46-8, 49, 50, 82
Cogan, Frank 110
Cowper, Earl 16
Cuffley 38, 54

Danesbury Approved School 67
Daniell, Henry 19
Desborough, Lord 46

Dyrham Park 65

Economic depression and unemployment 31, 41, 43, 44, 46, 55-6, 78-9
Education and schools 9, 13, 16-7, 18, 27-9, 32, 34-6, 38, 39, 40, 48, 52-4, 55-6, 64, 65, 68-72, 73, 74, 75, 79, 82-6, 102, 106, 108, 112-13
Enfield, London Borough of 53, 108
Essex 7, 40, 43, 77
Evans, John 14

Finance 7, 11, 17-18, 50, 82, 83-4, 108-109, 112
Fire and ambulance service 18, 55, 56, 58-61, 79, 82, 83, 90-92, 100, 108, 112
Flamstead 36

Gaddesden, Little 71
Gade Valley 13
Graveson, William 50

Hadham, Much 95; Hadham Palace 34; Hadham Hall 107
Hardiman, A F 49
Hardy, William Le 24; W J 25
Harpenden 41, 74
Harrow, London Borough of 108
Hatfield 9, 13, 17, 19, 46, 48, 64, 72, 90, 93, 101, 111, 113
Polytechnic 72, 73, 77, 85-6, 88, 108
Health and hospitals 9, 10, 16, 18, 25-6, 29, 38-9, 40, 48, 49, 55, 56, 59, 61, 64, 65-6, 67, 79, 82, 86, 89, 99, 100-102, 109, 112
Hemel Hempstead 29, 36, 62, 64, 67
Hertford 9, 10, 13, 14, 16, 19, 22, 25, 27, 34, 36, 38, 39, 46, 50, 59, 72, 74, 91, 98, 112
Balls Park 72, 85-6, 107
County Hall 25, 32, 46-9, 50, 52, 59, 73, 75, 106, 112
Shire Hall 16, 24, 25, 46-8, 107, 112
Hertfordshire 7, 9, 13, 31, 39, 43, 44, 46, 52, 53, 55, 64, 68-9, 74, 75, 78, 88, 111
Hertfordshire County Council 10, 11, 14, 16-17, 20, 21, 32, 46, 48, 50, 65-6, 80-83, 89, 107-109, 111, 112, 113
Members and Chairmen 14-16, 32, 33, 46, 54, 57, 80, 81, 111
Officers and Staff 17, 32, 46-50, 54, 67, 80, 82-3, 91, 101, 106, 108, 112, 113
Hillingdon, London Borough of 77
Hine, Reginald 106
Hirsch, Leonard 71
Hitchin 9, 13, 28, 36, 41, 43, 59, 65, 70-71, 99, 107
Hoddesdon 70, 74, 99

127

Holwell 89
Howard, Ebenezer 45, 64
Hunsdon 74
Huntingdonshire 10, 16, 25, 79

Ireton, Philip 80

James and Bywaters and Roland Pierce 48
Jellicoe, G A 64

Keen, William Brock 17, 50
Kent 21, 77
Knebworth 38, 46, 72

Leavesden 88
Lee Valley 45
Leeds 22
Letchworth 36, 45, 72, 74, 85, 98
Libraries, museums and the arts 16, 32, 36-8, 48, 56, 67, 72-4, 82, 98-100, 107, 108, 112, 113
Licensing and taxation (local) 10, 16, 20-21, 46, 48, 83
Lindgren, George 33
Local Government 7-11, 13-14, 18, 55-6, 66, 77, 78, 79, 80, 83, 84, 86, 98, 104
   Elections 7, 9, 10, 14, 32, 57, 78, 80-81, 111
London 13, 17, 19, 21, 33, 34, 44, 45-6, 46-8, 50, 64, 112
   London County Council 33, 46, 56, 64, 73, 75
   Greater London Council 56, 80, 96, 98
London Colney 63
Longmore, Sir Charles Elton 16, 17, 33, 49;
   Philip Elton 49-50
Lough, Stuart 92
Luton (Bedfordshire) 79

Manchester 79
Markyate 62-3
Middlesex 11, 17, 21, 25, 40, 56

Newsom, John 56, 68
Nicholson, Sir Richard 17
Norwich 48

Offley 36, 72
Oxhey 64, 73

Panshanger 13, 16
Party politics 14, 32-3, 57, 78, 79, 80-81, 111
Pickard, William 36
Pishiobury Approved School 67
Police 10, 16, 18, 19-20, 21, 48, 55, 56, 61-2, 79, 82, 83, 89-90, 92, 100-101, 112
Potters Bar 56, 111

Quarter Sessions 10-11, 13-14, 16, 17, 18, 19, 24, 25
Queen Elizabeth the Queen Mother 49

Radlett 95
Records and Record Office 24-5, 48, 82, 104-106, 112
Rickmansworth 13, 19, 44-45, 73, 107
Roads and bridges 7, 9, 10, 13, 14, 16, 17, 18-19, 24, 32, 44, 50, 55, 56, 58, 61-2, 62-3, 65, 83, 90, 92-5, 98, 100, 101, 108, 111-12
Royston 9, 40, 66, 70, 79, 85
Rushworth, W G 22

Sacombe 36
St Albans 9, 10, 13, 14, 16, 17, 19, 22, 25, 29, 30, 36, 39, 40, 41, 46, 61, 62, 63, 66, 67, 72, 74, 86, 98, 111, 115
   Court House 16, 17, 25, 30, 46-8, 112
Salisbury, Marquess of 16, 21, 46
Sandridge 38
Sawbridgeworth (Pishiobury) 67
Shaw, H Watkins 71
Shenley 65
Simpson, Evelyn 14
Smith, Urban 17
Social Services 25, 66, 68, 82-3, 86-9, 107, 108, 109, 112, 113
Stevenage 9, 59, 63, 64, 66, 67, 72, 74, 78, 84, 85, 96, 107
Suffolk 14, 108
Surveyor, County 17, 18, 46, 48, 49, 62, 74

Town and Country Planning 18, 44-6, 55, 56, 64-5, 82, 95-8, 109, 112
Treasurer, County 16, 17, 50
Tring 9, 79
Turnford 44

Uxbridge, Middlesex (Brunel University) 72

Walkern 59
Ware 9, 13, 38, 66, 92
Waste disposal 95, 102
Waterford 36
Watford 9, 13, 19, 22, 27, 29, 34, 36, 40, 43, 44, 52, 59, 62, 67, 71, 72, 88, 95, 98, 99, 102, 103
Watton-at-Stone 38, 96
Watson, Sylvia 56, 67
Weights and measures/Trading standards 10, 16, 21-4, 48, 82, 83, 102-5, 108, 112
Welfare and poor relief 7, 10, 18, 32, 33, 40-44, 48, 56, 65-8
Welham Green 96
Welwyn Garden City 45, 64, 70, 72, 73, 75, 90, 99, 111
Westmill 111
Willian 38
Woodhouse, Robert 33-4
World War (First) 29-30, 31, 38, 113;
   (Second) 32, 41, 50-4, 55, 57, 58, 69, 75, 113
Wrotham Park 65